CONCILIUM

Religion in the Eighties

CONCILIUM

Editorial Directors

Concilium 163 (3/1983): Dogma

MARTYRDOM TODAY

Edited by
Johannes-Baptist Metz
and
Edward Schillebeeckx

English Language Editor
Marcus Lefébure

T. & T. CLARK LTD.
Edinburgh

THE SEABURY PRESS
New York

March 1983
T. & T. Clark Ltd., 36 George Street, Edinburgh EH2 2LQ
ISBN: 0 567 30043 9

The Seabury Press, 815 Second Avenue, New York, NY 10017
ISBN: 0 8164 2443 8

Library of Congress Catalog Card No.: 82 062756

Printed in Scotland by William Blackwood & Sons Ltd., Edinburgh

Concilium: Monthly except July and August.
Subscriptions 1983: UK and Rest of the World £27·00, postage and handling included; USA and Canada, all applications for subscriptions and enquiries about *Concilium* should be addressed to The Seabury Press, 815 Second Avenue, New York, NY 10017, USA.

CONTENTS

Editorial

ECCLESIA MARTYRUM, Church of the martyrs—this is an old and honourable title that gives the clearest expression to the common fate which the Church shares with its Lord. 'Martyrdom today' is the heading of this issue. The purpose of this subject is to show that in talking of the 'Church of the martyrs' we are dealing not just with a historical but also with a contemporary reality, even if at least partially we have in this case interpreted the title a little more broadly and have in general discussed at length situations of persecution and oppression (not infrequently of Christians by Christians). The contributions to this issue are meant to offer a segment of contemporary ecclesiology and to work the Church's present history of suffering into the way in which dogmatic theology understands the Church.

In order to see and understand the contemporary Church as a Church of the martyrs, one must observe that there is something like a historical and cultural shift in the pattern of martyrdom and the image of the martyr. There is something like a shift from the 'heroic' to the 'anonymous' martyr, from individual martyrdom to a kind of collective martyrdom. The contributions that follow should help one to see this more clearly. And it is hoped that they will draw readers' attention to a contemporary form of political sanctity: to that which arises from an unconditional love for 'the least of the brethren' and in this follows the poor and suffering Jesus to the point of death. The articles by Jon Sobrino and Leonardo Boff are explicitly concerned with this contemporary pattern and image of martyrdom and sanctity: it also emerges in most of the 'biographical' contributions, while Karl Rahner, faced with this form of discipleship in suffering and being conformed to the pattern of Christ, pleads for an expansion or modification of the 'classical' understanding of martyrdom.

The issue begins with contributions dealing at a fundamental level with the concept and understanding of martyrdom in the tradition of the Bible and the Church, and thus with contributions concerned with studying the general theological criteria of martyrdom. To this group belong the article by Theofried Baumeister, the articles that have just been mentioned by Karl Rahner, Leonardo Boff and Jon Sobrino, and that by Francisco Claver. Beyond this the issue offers numerous theological reports on the actual experience of the widest possible variety of local churches and differing Christian surroundings. Because of recent years the relationship of the churches in what is termed the 'First World' to those in the 'Third World' has become one of the major theological concerns of this journal, we have included several reports on the situation in the poor churches of the Third World—as a sign of hope and challenge for the Church as a whole. In this category belong the contributions by Juan Hernández Pico, Maurice Barth and Pedro Casaldáliga. We are especially grateful for the opportunity of publishing the article by Vàclav Mali on the situation of the Church in Czechoslovakia. In this context Walbert Bühlmann inquires into the conduct today of Church institutions in situations of persecution, whether this is with regard to Eastern Bloc States or the countries of Latin America. On the basis of the history of his country's religious and political sufferings Enda McDonagh develops an 'Irish perspective' on the question of martyrdom. Desmond Tutu talks of the spirituality of suffering and the cross that enables one to bear Christian witness against apartheid and also to endure persecution by one's own brothers and sisters in the faith. Daniel Berrigan testifies to the motives and experience of his brand of radical Christian pacifisim. James Cone attempts to show the extent to which Martin Luther King's readiness to go to the limit and thus his readiness to die in the struggle for freedom of his Black sisters and brothers has its spiritual roots precisely in the tradition of the Black Church. Taking Martin Luther King into consideration has already meant an ecumenical broadening of our canvas. This applies, too, to the article by Georges Casalis on Dietrich Bonhoeffer, whose personality is for many Christians a powerful example of a theological existence subsumed under the heading of martyrdom. Because the idea of martyrdom today is above all linked with the fate of the Jews, we are grateful to Abel Herzberg for writing a contribution on martyrdom and the Holocaust.

Nowhere are doctrine and life, the history of ideas and biography so interwoven as in the question of martyrdom today. Hence in this issue theological and biographical data are continually merging into each other. Under the heading 'Martyrdom today' the Church of our time is confronted with its most painful and most hopeful experiences. But let us not forget that at the same time it is confronted by the scandal that consists of Christians persecuting Christians.

JOHANNES-BAPTIST METZ
EDWARD SCHILLEBEECKX

PART I

Ecclesiological and Dogmatic Reflections

Theofried Baumeister

Martyrdom and Persecution in Early Christianity

THE WAY in which the term martyr is taken for granted both inside and outside the Church can make us forget sometimes that the image of the martyr that we are used to represents a historical phenomenon which we can observe coming into being. The decisive step in the formation of the image of the Christian martyr was taken in the second century, almost certainly influenced by actual instances of martyrdom. Earlier the question of violent death for the sake of Christian conviction finds its place within the larger and more general question of the theological treatment of persecution. What can be established in the second century is how the case of persecution unto death is detached from every other form of persecution and the image of the martyr becomes sharply delineated. In the Church the same point is being reached that on the Jewish side was indicated by the accounts of martyrdom in 2 and 4 Maccabees (2 Macc. 6:18-7:42; the whole of 4 Macc.), which now influence the Christian view. The independence shown by the martyr and the search for a concise label are well illustrated in the Shepherd of Hermas, that apocalyptic penitential tract that was probably written in the decade AD 140 to 150. Those who have died for the sake of the faith Hermas describes for the most part as those 'who have suffered for the sake of the law' (using *páschein* in the aorist participle, *pathóntes*), and thus distinguishes them from those who have been persecuted (*thlibéntes*) but have not suffered, i.e., been killed (*Sim.* viii:3:6-7). The high regard in which the former are held is shown by their being given the place of honour above the visionary and the community's elders (*Vis.* iii:1:8-9).

Our usual terminology describes Christians persecuted unto death as martyrs (*mártures*) and their death as bearing witness (*marturein*) and martyrdom (*martúrion*). In extant literature we encounter this usage for the first time in the letter which the community at Smyrna wrote to that at Philomelion to describe—and interpret theologically—the death of their bishop Polycarp. There is no explanation of the terminology, which must therefore have been current in Asia Minor at the time the letter was written. In recent years there has been a vigorous debate over the dating of Bishop Polycarp's death. The difficulty arises from the apparent contradiction between the account of the letter itself (c. 21) and that given by Eusebius in his *Chronicles* and *Church History*. Recently Pierre Brind'Amour has put forward the plausible suggestion that the 'great sabbath' mentioned by the letter (c. 21) was not in fact a Saturday but a Sunday.[1] In this case there is nothing to stop us accepting Eusebius's dates and taking as

3

the date of Polycarp's death 23 February 167, which was in fact a Sunday. Hence the terminology of martyrdom must have come into use in Asia Minor in the decades leading up to 160, though on the evidence of the Shepherd of Hermas it was still unknown in Rome at this time.

How did the terminology of martyrdom, of bearing witness, come to be applied to the descriptions of violent death suffered for the sake of the faith? There has been an abundance of investigations into this question. Norbert Brox has shown that the usage did not gradually develop from the biblical terminology of witness.[2] In my view attention must be paid to a central group of ideas in the letters of Ignatius of Antioch: they may not contain this precise terminology, but they can be well understood as a preparatory phase before it took shape.[3] Ignatius repeatedly stresses that it is not enough to be called a Christian but that one must submit being a Christian to proof by what one does (*Magn.* 4 and elsewhere). This kind of action has in turn the character of verbal acknowledgement. Dying because one is a Christian is the action *par excellence* in which the disciple who is called to this confirms his or her faith by following the example of Jesus' suffering and through action is able once again to become a word with power to speak to others (see especially Ignatius *Rom.* 2:1). The demand that word and deed should coincide is also to be found in the Stoa and in popular philosophy. Ignatius linked it with the idea of dying for the sake of the faith. At the same time the concept includes a soteriological component inasmuch as the action of the disciple is accomplished within the reality of salvation that is constituted by the death of Christ: it is thus a transition from death to life with God. As Epictetus shows (*Diss.* iii:26, 28), the complex of ideas word-deed-word could without difficulty be linked with the word *mártus* or witness. As the technical term to describe a Christian who was killed this word became established first of all in Asia Minor and then throughout the rest of the Christian world. The distinction Hermas drew was maintained: the *homológetés* or confessor was distinguished from the martyr. But a certain imprecision could creep into the usage to the extent that the confessor could also be called a martyr. Indications of the original meaning of the terminological differentiation between martyr and confessor can be drawn from two extracts from the conclusion of the letter (quoted at length by Eusebius in his *Church History*) from the Christians of Vienne and Lyons about the persecution in their area in the year 177 (Eusebius HE v:1:2-4:3). Those who are merely imprisoned object to being called martyrs (HE v:2:2-3). In a martyrological interpretation of Rev. 1:5 and 3:14 the title is reserved for Christ and those who have sealed their witness through death. The description of Stephen as the perfect martyr (HE v:2:5) could be an allusion, taken in a martyrological sense, to Acts 22:20, which in the realm of ideas had become involved with the account of Stephen's martyrdom in Acts 6:8-7:60. It could indeed be that it was precisely the New Testament's use of the terminology of witness (*martureîn*) that was a reason for seeing it in a new light and applying it particularly to those among the persecuted who were regarded with the greatest respect. What was important was that irreproachable witness was borne in a martyr's death. We must always bear in mind that in a situation of persecution some people naturally shrank back from the ultimate that was demanded of them. Witness—and here we are still reminded of giving evidence in court—must therefore be ratified by death: only thus did someone become a witness, a *mártus*, in the full sense of the word. Confessors had such a test of their sincerity still ahead of them or were not required to submit to it. The term applied to them means above all the verbal acknowledgement they gave of being a Christian in the circumstances of imprisonment and suffering. The *Apostolic Tradition* of Hippolytus, dating from the early third century, includes a section on confessors.[4] They should not have hands laid on them to ordain them to the diaconate or presbyterate because they have already attained to the dignity of the presbyterate through their confession of faith. It is to be understood that they were regarded as charismatics, since the Holy Spirit had spoken through them in court (Mark 13:11 and parallel passages). In what follows it becomes clear who in the proper sense of the word should count as a confessor: not someone who happens to be treated with contempt or, probably as a slave, is subjected to domestic punishment, but someone who is put on trial, imprisoned and sentenced to punishment. It is clear that in retrospect prisoners are described as martyrs when it is known that they later died a martyr's death.

It is worth going back once again to the description of Polycarp's martyrdom in order to go beyond the question of terminology and grasp the image of martyrdom presented by this letter. What was written by the Christians of Smyrna is the first Christian document to have martyrdom as its exclusive subject. A comparison of the text as it has come down to us with the quotations and summary given by Eusebius in his *Church History* (HE iv:15:1-48) led Hans von Campenhausen to conclude that what had originally been a much simpler account had been subjected to successive later revisions.[5] The argument over this hypothesis confirmed the observation made by Giuseppe Lazzati that Eusebius's text omits the exhortatory passages.[6] Eusebius, in other words, simply edited and abridged the account: he is not a witness of another document than the one we have, which including its final remarks was written shortly after Polycarp's death. The parallel that is drawn between this martyrdom and the passion of Jesus thus belongs to the original document and is not the work of an editor. Here we encounter a continuation of the theme of discipleship to be found in the Synoptic Gospels. The correspondence between the situations is meant to make clear the community of fate in which Polycarp shows himself to be a true disciple who follows his master. It is thus a question of the twofold theme of the parallelism of the situations and of imitation as a recasting of the idea of discipleship to fit in with Greek ideas. The whole style of the report has Johannine characteristics. The author decodes earthly happenings to show that the consummation is already taking place: in the midst of their sufferings the martyrs are already living in the world of heaven. In the prayer just before his death with its eucharistic overtones, Polycarp offers himself as a sacrifice, gives thanks for the grace of martyrdom and glorifies God (see *Mart. Pol.* 14:3 with John 21:19). The occasional hints of the miraculous show that the Greek idea of the *theîos anér*, the divine man, had its influence on the image of the martyr. The respect and veneration paid to Polycarp while he was alive are continued after his death. The community's intention is to gather at his grave on the anniversary of his martyrdom (*Mart. Pol.* 18:3). Here it becomes clear how the theology of martyrdom became the seed-bed of the veneration of the martyrs which now arose and of which this passage in the *Martyrdom of Polycarp* is the earliest evidence.

Just before the *Martyrdom of Polycarp* was written the apologist Justin, who himself was to die a martyr's death, took up the subject of martyrdom without being aware of the terminology of witness or *martureîn*. He latches on to the image of the courageous philosopher facing those wielding power, an image common among the Stoics, Cynics and Platonists. His aim is to reclaim for the martyr the dignity of the persecuted friend of truth who, even if he appears to be defeated, is nevertheless in his frankness and sincerity (*parrhesía*) the true victor. In philosophical circles stories were told with a punch-line showing the philosopher fearless and undaunted. In this context one section of Socrates' *Apology* (Plato Ap. 30 C-D) was reduced to the sentence: 'Anytos and Meletos (Socrates' two accusers) may be able to kill me, but they cannot harm me.' In his first Apology Justin refers to this sentence (*Ap.* I:2:4) and indeed sees in Socrates a forerunner of the Christian martyrs. In the Dialogue with Trypho (Dial. 9:1) he declares that Christians will not be false to their convictions even when they encounter abuse and invective and the vilest of tyrants tries to force them to recant: he himself feared nobody, even if he were to be hacked into pieces on the spot by those present (Dial. 120:6). In the context of this view of martyrdom the entire conceptual world of military service and all the rhetoricians' praise for strength of character, as contained in the non-canonical fourth book of Maccabees, could be carried over to the martyrs. This laid the foundation for the legends of the martyrs and their honouring as Christian heroes, something which can be established from the fourth century on. However sceptical one may be towards many of the forms which arose in this way, the original sense of this kind of image of the martyr should not be overlooked. To the extent that one understood martyrdom as a moral victory, one changed the sign and took up the cause of the weak against arbitrary despotism. If the apocalyptic element looked to the future to bring about the transformation of a situation of injustice, then according to this way of thinking this kind of transformation already took place at the moment of suffering, itself transformed into a victory.

Up till now we have been following the way whereby the martyr became a clearly defined and prominent figure of the Church. One consequence of this development was that earlier ways in which theology coped with the situation of persecution were not pursued further or only in a very much altered form. But if today we are concerned to get a fresh grasp of the idea of martyrdom it is worth having a look at these early attempts in which the subject of violent death has not yet been isolated but appears in the wider context as the extreme case of rejection and persecution. Here of course we can only indicate a few of the basic ideas.[7] What was original and new in the Christian treatment of the subject of persecution is based on the historical situation of Jesus, the group of disciples and the early Christian communities. What Jesus asked of his disciples when they experienced rejection was that, in unconditional attachment to him and participating in his service to God's rule, they should not evade the rejection he encountered. Nothing, not even saving one's own life, should be given precedence over loyalty to Jesus and the obedience this showed to the will of God. Looking back after Easter on Jesus' death, this demand could be more strongly emphasised as the idea of following and imitating the crucified one. Probably the earliest attempt to make sense of rejection was the reference to the fate of the prophets. In Jesus' day the idea was in circulation that not just this prophet or that but all prophets had died a violent death as a result of what they had done. A statement along these lines was originally used to serve the preaching of repentance, but in cases where it was applied to their own experience by those affected it could illuminate the fate they were suffering.

Another Jewish theme re-interpreted in early Christian circles was the apocalyptic argument. The book of Daniel shows that the job of apocalyptic was to offer help in a situation of oppression. At the time of religious confusion during the reign of the Syrian King Antiochus IV Epiphanes (BC 175-163) the writer looks into the future. If the depths of human malice are plumbed in the actions of this king in the near future, God brings about the great revolution in which justice is restored (see especially Dan. 11:21-12:4). The writer extracts a meaning from the fate of those who have been killed before that happens: their death serves to test and purify (Dan. 11:35). In apocalyptic writings images are developed of resurrection and final judgment with the rewarding of those who have been persecuted and the punishment of those who did the persecuting, in which the oppressed are able to play an active part, as well as the idea of a different intermediate state. The justified basic concern behind all these attempts is the determination not simply to come to terms with and accept the injustice that exists in the world. Through believing in the justice of God one knows that oppression cannot be the last word. On the Christian side this idea was taken over with the decisive modification that the Son of Man, Jesus, had a central position. One's attitude to Jesus and his messengers is decisive for one's fate at the judgment of the Son of Man. The end is preceded by a time of confusion and persecution in which it is a matter of remaining true to faith in Jesus.

In distinction to the Jewish treatment of persecution the corresponding Christian statements often occur in connection with proclamation and mission. The link between the two can reach the point that the scene of judgment itself takes on the character of proclamation (Mark 13:9-11 and parallel passages, the court scenes in Acts). The messengers in the *logia* source used by Matthew and Luke who carry on Jesus' preaching of the kingdom of God (see Luke 10:9b) are compared to sheep who are sent among wolves (Luke 10:3). Anyone who rejects their greeting automatically cuts himself or herself off from the peace to be bestowed at the end of time (Luke 10:5-6). Those who reject them will be punished by being themselves repudiated at the end of time (Luke 10:10-12).

A special place in the letters of Paul is taken up by the subject of suffering that is connected with the situation of proclaiming the Gospel.[8] The suffering that Paul has to put up with in his apostolic ministry is understood by him on the basis of his preaching of the cross as sharing the same fate with the crucified one with the aim of thereby gaining a share in Jesus' risen life. The power of God is at work in human weakness (2 Cor. 12:9), and initially this power shows itself in the experience of being saved (2 Cor. 4:7-11). Within the limitations of the apocalyptic interpretation of the end of time, to which suffering belongs, salvation is granted in Jesus' cross and resurrection, and this salvation is already present here and now as divine life in suffering so that it can become completely manifest. Paul can rejoice in the midst of persecution (Phil. 2:18). Death has lost its terrors: it is the gateway to being with Christ (Phil. 1:23). Paul opposes an enthusiastic overemphasis of suffering. His view of suffering is distinct from Stoic impassivity and from an apocalyptic thinking in terms of reward and mere consolation. Suffering is something oppressive, but God's power can be discerned in it as the beginning of future glory. Occasionally the apostle talks specifically of his suffering as an apostle. But his interpretation applies just as well to the community's experience of suffering. In the context of this approach persecution can be praised as good (see 1 Peter 1:6-9, 4:12-19).

Here we cannot go into all aspects of the way persecution and suffering are treated in the writings of the New Testament. The aim has been merely to make clear how rich a world of ideas is to be found from which the thread of the theology of martyrdom in the strict sense has emerged. The prominence given to the martyrs should not be made retrospective. But those others who suffer besides the martyrs should not be overlooked. Today they need a different theological treatment than in early Christianity.

Translated by Robert Nowell

Notes

1. P. Brind'Amour 'La Date du martyre de Saint Polycarpe (Le 23 février 167)' in *Analecta Bollandiana* 98 (1980) 456-462.

2. N. Brox *Zeuge und Märtyrer. Untersuchungen zur frühchristlichen Zeugnis-Terminologie* (Munich 1961 (bibliography)).

3. T. Baumeister *Die Anfänge der Theologie des Martyriums* (Münster 1980) pp. 257-270.

4. Reconstructed by B. Botte *La Tradition apostolique de saint Hippolyte* (Münster 1966) p. 28.

5. H. von Campenhausen 'Bearbeitungen und Interpolationen des Polykarpmartyriums' in *Sitzungsberichte der Akademie Heidelberg (Phil.-hist. Klasse)* (1957) pp. 5-48, and in his *Aus der Frühzeit des Christentums* (Tübingen 1963) pp. 253-301.

6. G. Lazzati 'Nota su Eusebio epitomatore di atti dei martiri' in *Studi in onore di A. Calderini e R. Paribeni* (Milan 1956) I pp. 377-384 (the reference is to p. 380). See also L. W. Barnard 'In defence of Pseudo-Pionius' account of Saint Polycarp's martyrdom' in *Kyriakon. Festschrift J. Quasten* (Münster 1979) I pp. 193-204, and B. Dehandschutter *Martyrium Polycarpi. Een literair-kritische studie* (Louvain 1979) pp. 131-155.

7. On what follows, see the book mentioned in note 3.

8. *Ibid.*, especially pp. 187-191.

Karl Rahner

Dimensions of Martyrdom:
A Plea for the Broadening of a
Classical Concept

THE AIM of this article is to plead for a certain broadening of the traditional concept of martyrdom.

As it is used in the Church today, this traditional concept is well known. We are not concerned here with the question how it has developed in the course of the Church's history, what its relationship is to the biblical concept of martyrdom, or once again what the connection is between this New Testament concept and various related concepts and ideas such as proclamation, prophecy, confession, and death. Here we presuppose the concept of martyrdom that is traditional in the Church today: what is meant by this concept of dogmatic and fundamental theology is the free, tolerant acceptance of death for the sake of the faith, except in the course of an active struggle as in the case of soldiers. Faith includes Christian moral teaching, as, for example, is clearly shown by the fact that the Church honours as a martyr St Maria Goretti, who was stabbed to death in 1902 by a young man belonging to a neighbouring family because she vigorously resisted his advances. Faith can involve the entirety of the Christian confession of faith or merely one single truth of Christian teaching on faith and morals, though of course this one single truth is always understood within the context of the entirety of the Christian message. Death *in odium fidei* must be consciously accepted, so that a distinction must be drawn between martyrdom and baptism of blood. What is specific about this concept is that as far as the Church is concerned today it excludes death in an active struggle. Our question therefore is whether this kind of exclusion of a death suffered in active struggle for the Christian faith and its moral demands (including those affecting society as a whole) must necessarily and always be linked with the concept of martyrdom. This question is of considerable weight for the life of individual Christians and of the Church, because the recognition of martyrdom with regard to a Christian engaged in an active struggle or fight would mean a significant official recommendation by the Church of this kind of active struggle as an example worthy of imitation by other Christians.

To begin with it is obvious that concepts like the one we are dealing with here have a history and may legitimately vary. All that is involved is the question whether in this case tolerating and enduring death for the sake of the faith and enduring death in an active struggle for the faith (or for this or that of its demands) cannot be included under the single concept of martyrdom: both types of death share a wide-ranging and profound content in common, and bracketing the two in this kind of single concept would not deny a lasting difference between them. There are many concepts that bring two realities together because they in fact resemble each other without thereby denying or necessarily obscuring differences between them. (The concept 'sin' is used within the Church jointly for our inherited corruption and for the state of sin for which we are personally responsible, without any intention of denying a radical distinction between these two states of affairs.) It is of course correct that patiently enduring death for the sake of faith has a special relationship to the death of Jesus, who precisely by the death he endured has become the faithful and reliable witness *par excellence*. But this undeniable distinction between these two kinds of death does not exclude their being brought together under the single concept and term of martyrdom.

Much needs to be considered in order to see this and to bring out the inner and essential similarity between these two kinds of death alongside all the differences between them. First of all, the death Jesus 'passively endured' was the consequence of the struggle he waged against those in his day who wielded religious and political power. He died because he fought: his death must not be seen in isolation from his life. Putting this argument the other way around, someone who dies while fighting actively for the demands of his or her Christian convictions (which of course in certain circumstances can include the demands made on society as a whole) can also be said patiently to endure his or her death. It is not a death directly sought in itself. It includes a passive element, just as the death of a martyr in the usual sense includes an active element, since by his or her active witness and life this kind of martyr has conjured up the situation in which he or she can only escape death by denying his or her faith. The question may of course remain of how active struggle is to be more closely defined and marked off from similar activities so that death in this kind of active struggle can and should be treated as martyrdom. It is not everyone who dies on the Christian or more narrowly Catholic side in a religious war who should be described as a martyr. In practice in religious wars of this kind too many secular motives are included, and the question remains open whether everyone fighting in such wars was really prepared for his or her death and really accepted it. But, for example, why should not someone like Bishop Romero, who died while fighting for justice in society, a struggle he waged out of the depths of his conviction as a Christian—why should he not be a martyr? Certainly he was prepared for his death.

We should not simply conceive of passively tolerating one's death only in the manner we are used to in the case of early Christian martyrs brought before a court and sentenced to death. There are quite different ways in which the passive but intentionally accepted toleration of death can occur. Contemporary persecutors of Christians do not give their victims any opportunity to confess their faith in the style of the earliest Christian centuries and to accept a death to which they are sentenced by a court. But nevertheless their death in these more anonymous forms of contemporary persecution of Christians can still be foreseen and accepted just as in the case of the old-style martyr. And indeed it can be foreseen and accepted as the consequence of an active struggle for justice and other Christian realities and values. What is in fact strange is that the Church has canonised Maximilian Kolbe as a confessor and not as a martyr. An unprejudiced approach would pay more attention to how he behaved in the concentration camp and at his death than to his earlier life and would see him as a martyr of selfless Christian love.

In any case the distinctions between a death for the sake of the faith in active struggle for this faith and death for the sake of the faith in passive endurance are too fleeting and too difficult to define for one to have to go to the trouble of maintaining a precise conceptual and verbal apartheid between these two kinds of death. Underlying both is ultimately the same explicit and decided acceptance of death for the same Christian reasons. In both cases death is the acceptance of the death of Christ, an acceptance which as the supreme act of love and fortitude puts the believer totally at God's disposal, which represents the most radical unity in action of love and of enduring the ultimate helplessness in the face of man's incomprehensible yet effective rejection of God's self-revealing love. In both cases death appears as quite simply the perfect and public manifestation of the real essence of Christian death. Even when death is suffered in the struggle for Christian belief it is the witness of faith based on absolute determination springing from the grace of God, a determination that seeks to integrate the whole of existence up to and beyond death, in the midst of the most profound inward and outward powerlessness that the person concerned accepts with patience. This applies, too, to death in battle because, just like the passive martyr in the traditional sense, this fighter experiences and endures the power of evil and his own powerlessness in the experience of his outward failure.

In this plea for a certain broadening of the traditional concept of martyrdom we can appeal to Thomas Aquinas. Thomas says that someone is martyr through a death that is clearly related to Christ if he is defending society (*res publica*) against the attacks of its enemies who are trying to damage the Christian faith and if in this defence he suffers death (In IV Sent. dist. 49 q. 5 a. 3 quaest. 2 ad 11). Damage to the Christian faith as is opposed by this kind of defender of society can of course be concerned with a single dimension of Christian belief, because otherwise even the passive toleration of death for the sake of a single demand of Christian faith or morals could not be termed martyrdom. In this way in his commentary on the Sentences Thomas is defending a more comprehensive concept of martyrdom such as is proposed here.

A legitimate 'political theology', a theology of liberation, should concern itself with this enlargement of the concept. It has a very down-to-earth practical significance for a Christianity and a Church that mean to be aware of their responsibility for justice and peace in the world.

Leonardo Boff

Martyrdom: An Attempt at Systematic Reflection

AS GENERALLY understood, martyrs are those who undergo violent death in witness to a religious truth or on account of practices which derive from this religious truth.[1] A theological reflection with pretensions to being systematic needs to pose the following questions: Why are there martyrs? What view of life lies behind martyrdom? The answers to these simple questions will lead us into a systematic reflection on the subject.

In the first place, martyrdom is possible because there are those who prefer to sacrifice their very lives rather than be unfaithful to their own convictions. The martyr has absolutes; situations can arise where his conscience requires acceptance of persecution and the sacrifice of his life in witness to the truth.

In the second place, martyrdom is possible because there are those who reject proclamation and denunciation; they persecute, torture and kill. That this is so simply demonstrates the fact of the general presence of evil in history. Truth, justice and God himself are not evident and do not regulate the relationships between individuals and societies. There also exist mechanisms of domination and falsehood, implying the denial of God. In such circumstances, to proclaim God, truth and justice can only be done, without betrayal and sin, through persecution and death. There have always been martyrs in history. Jesus of Nazareth belongs to this tradition of martyrdom. The Church, following Christ, not only has martyrs, but is a Church of martyrs. Martyrdom belongs to the true concept of the Church.[2] Its real function is not fidelity to a body of doctrine, but fidelity of life with Jesus who suffered persecution and martyrdom.

This attempt at systematic reflection will follow this outline: first, a consideration of Jesus Christ as the martyr *par excellence*; then, of the martyrs of the Christian faith, those who followed the martyr Jesus; finally, those martyrs for the kingdom of God, those who without belonging to explicit Christianity, nevertheless belong to the cause that was Christ's, the kingdom; they laid down their lives for those values that embody the Utopia of the kingdom, such as truth, justice, love of God and of the poor.

1. JESUS CHRIST, THE BASIC SACRAMENT OF MARTYRDOM

Jesus was put to a violent death because of his message and his practice. It can be read in different ways: as punishment for blasphemy and contempt for the law

(Pharisees); as the failure of a subversive and revolutionary political course (Romans); as the price paid for liberating and saving mankind. The early Christian communities, using themes and images from the Old Testament, tried to explain the religious and salvific significance of the life and fate of Jesus. So they saw him as the suffering just man, the servant who takes on the sins of others and suffers for them, the persecuted prophet and also the martyr-witness.[3] He is referred to as 'the faithful and true witness' (Rev. 1:5, 3:14) in the double classical meaning of the word: he who gives *oral* witness before the tribunal (cf. 1 Tim. 6:13) and he who witnesses through an *action*, accepting persecution and death (cf. Rev. 1:5). It would seem that the original version of Mark's Gospel put its account of the trial and condemnation of Jesus in the form of an *Acta Martyrum*, inspired by the acts of Hellenic martyrs and those of late Judaism.[4]

Jesus is presented, especially in the *Acta Martyrum*, as the prototype martyr.[5] The Christian martyrs were seen as following Christ the martyr, hence the description of Polycarp as '*socius Christi*'.[6] There is no space here to go into the martyr aspect of the Christ event, which has been dealt with at length elsewhere.[7] The martyr perspective becomes apparent from the moment when Jesus' message and actions begin to provoke a crisis in the different strata of Judaism: this is what leads to the incomprehension, the defamations, the threats of death. Jesus did not go unsuspectingly to his death. He courageously took on that risk; in his final period he hid himself from the temple police, but he made no concessions to the danger of his situation; he remained radically faithful to his message, to the Father and to the course he had chosen. He did not avoid his adversaries, nor flee from the crisis in Galilee, but 'resolutely took the road for Jerusalem' (Luke 9:51) for the final confrontation.

The accounts of Gethsemane and the Passion show Jesus' courage underlying the whole process; his resigned acceptance of the cross (see Luke 23:46) is a victory over the temptation to despair (see Mark 15:34). Early in the apostolic era, the image emerged of Jesus as patient sufferer, an example to all who suffer unjustly on account of their conscience in relation to God (see 1 Pet. 2:19): 'He was insulted and did not retaliate with insults; when he was tortured he made no threats but put his trust in the righteous judge' (1 Pet. 2:23). Jesus' martyrdom has to be understood correctly.[8] It was not a simple concordance with the will of God; historically it was the result of a rejection of his message and person by those who refused to be converted to the kingdom of God. If Jesus was to be faithful to himself and to his mission, he had to accept persecution and martyrdom. God did not want so much the death of his Son as the fidelity implied, in the context of men's refusal to be converted, by his violent death. This viewpoint is important for understanding martyrdom theologically, since this is never something sought in itself, but violently imposed from outside. As St Augustine said: 'It is not the punishment but the cause that makes true martyrs.'[9] The martyr defends not his life, but his cause, which is his religious conviction, his fidelity to God or his brother. And he defends this cause by dying.[10] The martyr poses a radical question: What is the ultimate meaning of that life which is sacrificed for something believed to be greater than life? The resurrection of the martyr Jesus Christ has, among others, this theological significance: who loses his life in this way receives it in fullness. To the martyr is reserved full participation in the meaning of life, that is, enthronement in its immortal kingdom.

2. MARTYRS OF THE CHRISTIAN FAITH: FOLLOWING AND PARTICIPATION

Jesus in his preaching summed up the main elements of martyrdom: 'You will be hated by all men on account of my name . . . you will be dragged before governors and kings for my sake . . . the disciple is not superior to his teacher . . .' (see Matt. 10:17-36).

Following Christ, as the best expression of the Christian faith, implies participating in his life and, ultimately, in his fate. The Christian martyrs of the early centuries understood this well, as the *Acta Martyrum* abundantly testify.[11] Christians found themselves confronted with a terrible dilemma: God (Christ) or Caesar.[12] Through being martyrs (witnesses) to the resurrection (see Acts 1:12, 2:32, 3:15, 13:31, 22:15. 26:16; 1 Cor. 9:1) like the Apostles, they bore witness to Jesus as the only Lord and God. In doing so they committed a crime of *lèse-majesté* against the Emperor (*asebeia*) by denying his status as a god; in consequence they also rejected all the Roman deities (*atheōtes*). So the Christian faith became politically subversive, since it attacked the foundations of the political-religious apparatus of the Empire and its leaders.[13]

So there are martyrs because of their public profession of a faith that de-absolutises and de-divinises the powers of this world, which claim to be the final arbiters. History is full of such martyrs, from the time the Roman emperors were declared divine to those who speak out against modern Fascist tyrannies.

There are likewise martyrs on account of their Christian practice derived from following Christ. Formerly, Christians undertook actions, *in recto* religious, which had political consequences; today, more and more Christians, particularly in the Third World, are carrying out actions, *in recto* political, which originate in faith and the Gospel. Not a few Christians (cardinals, bishops, priests, religious and lay people), because of the Gospel, make a preferential option for the poor, for their liberation, for the defence of their rights. In the name of this option they stand up and denounce the exercise of domination and all forms of social dehumanisation. They may be persecuted, arrested, tortured and killed. They, too, are martyrs in the strict sense of the word.[14]

Odium fidei is also apparent in their case. It is not simply their faith that is hated, but that particular type of liberating faith-praxis, inspired by passion for God and for the poor whom God loves. Christians are not, normally, hated because they call themsélves Christians. They are persecuted and hated because they commit themselves to the process of liberation and confess that this commitment comes from their experience of the Gospel and of prayer. It is this connection that is rejected and that provokes the sacrifice of their lives through martyrdom.

St Thomas Aquinas, tackling the question whether dying for the common good could be martyrdom, said with great theological acumen: 'Human good can become divine good if it is referred to God; therefore any human good can be a cause of martyrdom, in so far as it is referred to God'.[15] This is precisely the case of the numberless Christians involved in the liberation of their brothers, who refer their actions to God and to their following of Jesus Christ. They are no less martyrs than those who, before a Roman tribunal, proudly and fearlessly confessed '*Christianus sum*' and joyfully accepted their death.

3. MARTYRS FOR THE KINGDOM OF GOD: GOD'S POLICY

These die not in the name of explicit Christian faith, nor even in the name of practice derived from faith. Many give their lives in social processes of change which tend towards greater participation and justice for all.[16] Victorious revolutions (as in Cuba or Nicaragua) celebrate their heroes and martyrs who fell in defence of the humble or somewhere on the hard road to liberation. These become shining examples which inspire the spirit of revolution or the building of a new society. They chose the hardest way and have their own merit, regardless of any religious reference in their actions.

One may ask: What theological status do these political martyrs have, and can they really be called martyrs? I think they can be so called, in strict theological terms, and not as a euphemism. Origen rightly said: 'Anyone who witnesses to the truth, whether through words or through actions, has the right to be called a martyr; but among the brethren, inspired by their reverence for those who resisted even to death, the custom was established of calling martyrs those who witnessed to the mystery of faith with the spilling of their blood.'[17] This clearly sets out the essential and general quality required (witness to the truth) and the particular application worked out by consensus (bloody witness to the Christian truth). To the objection that, 'only faith in Christ gives those who suffer the glory of martyrdom', St Thomas replied: 'Christians are those who are of Christ; it is said of someone that he is of Christ not only because he has faith in Christ, but also because he performs virtuous actions in the spirit of Christ.'[18] So belonging to Christ is not to be found only through the way of conscience leading to an explicit act of faith; there is also an ontological reference to the extent that acts belong to the same spirit that inspired the actions of Christ. Christ's life was a pro-life, given over to the service of others and to unconditional fidelity to the truth and to God. As we have seen in the earlier quotation from St Thomas, any human good can be a cause of martyrdom, in so far as it is referred to God. This reference to God should be understood in its fullest sense; it is not only to be found in the simple act of consciously referring to something of God; a virtuous act in itself, by its ontic structure, contains reference to the principle of all virtue which is God. Objectively, that means, anything can consciously be referred to God.

Theology possesses categories for distinguishing God's presence where it is not proclaimed *as* God's presence. I am speaking now not of the Church but of the kingdom of God or the mystery of salvation. The kingdom and the mystery of salvation are theological realities which run through the Church and society; they appear under different signs, but in real and objective form. This is God entering into the matter of history and carrying out his word. And the true name of God is justice, love, peace without qualification; true faithfulness to God—and this in the end is what counts for salvation—is faithfulness to truth, justice and the requirements of peace. Therefore, all those who have died, and those yet to die, for these causes, regardless of their ideological allegiance, are truly martyrs through the spilling of their blood because they perform virtuous actions in the spirit of Christ. They are not martyrs of the Christian faith, not heroes of the Church; they are martyrs of the kingdom of God, martyrs to the cause that was the cause of the Son of God when he was in our midst. They help to carry out God's policy in history.

This radical and ontic perspective gives us the key to the essence of martyrdom, though there is no space here to enlarge on the fate of all those who suffer the same fate as Jesus. The poor, the oppressed races, natives, proletariat all share in his passion; the oppressions under which they live cut their lives off in their prime, kill their sons through spiritual and material poverty. This whole weight of injustice, charged with suffering and tears, is not without meaning and without fruit before God. The theology of the Suffering Servant and the sacrificed Messiah, the collective liberator of his people, enables us to see a divine and redeeming meaning in the midst of such contradiction.[19] Perhaps God's continuing mercy to the world in which we live depends on the intercession of these anonymous sufferers throughout history.

4. THE SACRAMENTAL VALUE OF MARTYRDOM

Martyrdom undoubtedly possesses an important function as sign (sacrament). It is primarily meaningful in an anthropological sense. What gives dignity to life is not self-centredness but outgoingness and the structure of pro-life. The martyr carries this life-dynamic to its most radical conclusion: total giving to the other through the gift of his own life. This gesture inevitably involves the question of what is of absolute value.

Normally, life is regarded as the supreme value, but the sacrifice of life through martyrdom points to something which is of a still higher value. In other words: life is ordered to something greater and more worthy. Other people? Society? Christian faith speaks of God; other people and society for whose good someone sacrifices himself carry on the same sphere of life; this means they cannot adequately represent the supreme value of life; other people and society are signs (sacraments) of God, the true name for the supreme meaning of life and of history. Martyrdom points up the relative nature of everything, even life itself—relative in a double sense: everything is related to a greater good for whose sake everything can be, and sometimes should be, sacrificed; compared to this greater good, all things are secondary or even tertiary, and so relative. The martyr signposts (and so is in himself a sacrament) the direction in which language which speaks of the absolute can be meaningful.

The martyr, through his courageous act, becomes a sacrament of the truth. This raises questions, as St Justin, Tertullian and the author of the *De Laude Martyrum* show: 'There is here something to study, a courage which needs to be investigated to its depths; we need to take note of a belief for which someone suffers and accepts death.'[20] It is not for nothing that the blood of martyrs is said to be the seed of new Christians.[21]

Finally, the martyr is an effective sacrament producing truth for the Church. The Church has martyrs and they are its glory. But whenever a Christian, in following Christ, commits himself in such a way that he is martyred for this, he lends credibility to the Church. More than this, he gives substance to the Church in the sense that a Church is only a Church of Christ in the degree to which it is prepared to live in such a way that it sees its normal practice as sharing the fate of the martyr Jesus Christ. The martyr makes the truth of the Church and reveals God's holiness communicated to the Church. The Church is holy because of its saints.

5. CONCLUSION

This short study has been designed to help understanding of the meaning of martyrdom from a systematic viewpoint. Martyrs are all those who suffer violent death for the sake of God or of Christ, or for the sake of actions derived from faith in God or in Christ; or, finally, for the sake of what constitutes the true content of the words God or Christ: truth and justice. Of course we need ways of surely identifying real truth and justice from the mechanisms of ideology (illusion), fanaticism (exacerbation of subjectivity) and idolatry (erroneous identification of God). Justice and truth constitute the absolute minimum of cause, without which those who are killed violently cannot be called martyrs. Truth and justice (the true name of God) are not so hidden that they cannot be discovered. The existence of martyrs proves their identity in history and in conscience.

Translated by Paul Burns

Notes

1. The following studies from the Catholic side can be considered classics: H. Delahaye 'Martyr et confesseur' in *Analecta Bollandiana* 39 (1921) 20-49; E. Hocedez 'Le Concept de martyr' in *NRTh* 55 (1928) 81-99, 198-208. On the Protestant side: F. Kattenbusch 'Der Märtyrtitel' in *ZNW* 4 (1903) pp. 111-127; K. Holl 'Der ursprüngliche Sinn des Namens Märtyrer' in *Neue Jahrbücher* 35 (1916) 353-359; R. Reintzenstein 'Der Titel Märtyrer' in *Hermes* 52 (1917) 442-452.

2. See E. Peterson 'Zeuge der Wahrheit' in *Theologische Traktate* (Munich 1951) pp. 167-224, esp. p. 175; *idem* 'Martirio e Martire' in *Enc. Catt.* VIII (Rome 1952) pp. 233-236.

3. See M.-L. Gubler *Die frühesten Deutungen des Todes Jesu* (Göttingen 1977) esp. pp. 10-94, 203-205.

4. See D. Dormeyer *Die Passion Jesu als Verhaltensmodel* (Munster 1974) esp. pp. 43-50, 238-261.

5. See *Les Chrétiens de Vienne et de Lyon à leurs frères d'Asie . . . Lettre sur les martyrs de 1977* eds. C. Montdesert and J. Comby (Lyons 1978) ch. 2, n. 3; other witnesses in Hocedez in the article cited in note 1, at pp. 200-201.

6. *Martyrium Sancti Polycarpi* VI; see *ibid*. XV.

7. See L. Boff *Jesucristo y la liberación del hombre* (Madrid 1981) pp. 316-363; H. Cousin *Le Prophète assassiné* (Paris 1976) pp. 221-230.

8. J. Sobrino *Christología desde América Latina* (Mexico 1976) pp. 79-185.

9. *In Ps.* 34; *Sermo* 2, 13. In PL 36, 340.

10. See *Actas de los Mártires* (Madrid 1951) 1149.

11. Delahaye, in the article cited in note 1, at pp. 46-47; Hocedez *op. cit.* pp. 200-203.

12. B. Reicke 'The Inauguration of Catholic Martyrdom according to St John the Divine' in *Augustinus* 20 (1980) 275-283, esp. p. 283.

13. I. Lesbeaupin *A bem-aventurança da perseguicão* (Petrópolis) pp. 13-18.

14. St Thomas Aquinas *In Ep. ad Rom. c. 8, lect.* 7: 'Patitur etiam propter Christum non solum qui patitur propter fidem Christi, sed etiam qui patitur pro quocumque iustitiae opere pro amore Christi.'

15. See 2a. 2ae. Q. 124 ad 3.

16. See *La sangre por el pueblo: Nuevos mártires de América Latina* (Petrópolis 1982); W. Bartz 'Heroische Heiligkeit und Martyrium ausserhalb der Kirche' in *Einsicht und Glaube* (Freiburg 1962) pp. 321-331.

17. *In Joan. II* in PG 14, 176.

18. 2a. 2ae. Q. 124, art. 5.

19. C. Mesters *O destino do povo que sofre* (Petrópolis 1981).

20. Justin *Apol.* II, 12: Tertullian *Ad Scapulam* 5; *De Laude Martyrum* 5.

21. Tertullian *Apol.* 50: 'Plures efficimur quoties metimur a vobis, semen est sanguis christianorum.'

Jon Sobrino

Political Holiness: A Profile

1. RELATION BETWEEN HOLINESS AND POLITICS

THE EXPRESSION *political holiness*[1] may seem odd, even nowadays, because it links two realities which are normally presumed to be separate not just in fact but because they ought to be. It is also an ambiguous expression until we explain clearly what we mean by both of the terms. In general, which is enough for this article, we mean by holiness the outstanding practice of faith, hope and, especially charity and the virtues generated by the following of Jesus. By politics we mean action directed towards structurally transforming society in the direction of the Kingdom of God, by doing justice to the poor and oppressed majorities, so that they obtain life and historical salvation.

Linking these two things means taking two new steps. The first is the presenting of a new environment for holiness as both possible and necessary. Throughout the history of the Church, it has been assumed that the proper environment for holiness is personal ascesis, contemplation, the exercise of charity in the form of almsgiving, etc. Now, because they have become aware of the misery and oppression of the majority of the human race and of the processes of liberation which have been set in motion in the Third World (with their analogies in the First World in the form of resistance to dictatorships, efforts at democratisation, etc.), many Christians feel that the area of political action is the right place to seek holiness. This of course does not exclude other ways of seeking holiness, but politics is one possible way and because of the signs of the times it has become a historical necessity.

The second more recent step, which was taken because of Christians' experiences of political involvement, means that now we are not talking about linking faith and politics merely, Christianity and politics, analysing their theoretical compatibility, the need for political involvement in the name of faith, but of linking *holiness* and politics. This stage has been reached, we believe, because Christians have realised two things: (*a*) In order to live a Christian political life it is not enough to be theoretically clear about its possibility and legitimacy; we have to practise and create specifically Christian values in an outstanding manner; (*b*) holiness is necessary for political action in order to avoid the negative subproducts inherent in this action and in order to make this action historically effective.

Thus politics today offers a sphere for holiness and holiness makes political action more humanising for those engaged in it and for the political project in which they are

18

engaged. This is what we want to show in this article, and we base our claim on the actual existence of this type of holiness and not on a merely conceptual analysis.

2. A HOLINESS WHICH REQUIRES POLITICS

'A religion held with deep conviction leads to political involvement and tends to create conflicts in a country like ours where there is a crying need for social justice' (Mons. Romero, 15.2.1980).[2]

(a) The development of Christian holiness always presupposes that it is in answer to God's will. This may be different for different people, but it must, essentially, include what is God's clear will in a particular moment of history. At the moment, as Medellín and Puebla remind us, God's primary will is that the poor majority should have life, that they should 'build houses and live in them, plant vines and eat their fruits' (Isa. 65;21). Or to put it in negative terms: that the poverty and oppression of millions of human beings should stop, that there should be an end to their constant deprivation of human dignity, the horrible violation of their rights, the massacres, mass expulsions, arrests, tortures and murders. The response to this primary will of God is a specific type of love for people, which does not exhaust other forms of love but is not reducible to them either: love for people most deprived of life and working so that they may have life, in the words of Mons. Romero, 'defend the minimum which is God's greatest gift: life'. This love, which is both a response to God's will and to the present enormous suffering of humanity, is what we call political love.

This political love has certain specific characteristics which differentiates it from other forms of love. In this first place it requires a *metanoia* to see the truth of the world as it is, in the manifestations of death, which are visible, and its structural causes, which are hidden and take care to be hidden, to see in this generalised death the largest fact and the most serious problem of humanity, the one which is the greatest challenge to the meaning of history and humanity, so that we do not imprison the truth of things through injustice (Rom. 1:18). It requires *pity* for the unhealed but not unhealable suffering of the oppressed majority, Jesus' pity for the multitude. It requires an awareness of *responsibility* when asked the question, 'what have you done with your brother?' (Gen. 4:95) and co-responsibility for his condition and his destiny. This co-responsibility also allows people to start recovering their dignity by sharing the suffering of humanity.

Political love tries to be *effective*. This means it must be expressed in a fitting manner to try to eradicate the death and bring about the life of the poor. To understand how this love can be effective we have to think first of those to whom this love wants to offer itself. These are the poor considered as a collectivity, group or social class, not the poor individual but the *polis*, the world of the poor. They are the poor in the material sense. What needs to be eradicated is not just the inner shame to which they are subjected but their material poverty. Moreover they are poor because of and in opposition to the powerful. They are dialectically poor and in conflict by their very existence.[3]

The political love which seeks to transform the situation of *these* poor people must have its specific mechanisms, distinct from those belonging to other forms of love; it must seek structural efficacy. It must denounce oppression and unmask its structural causes, plead for basic human social and political rights, help to bring about 'bold and urgent' structural changes, as Paul VI said.

It must also see the poor not only as the *objects* of beneficial political actions but also—especially now in many Third World countries—the enactors of their own destiny as a people fighting for liberation; *they* have the largest share in this struggle and must direct it objectively towards the creation of a new society. For this reason political love must also share—in very different ways—in the struggle of the poor, which takes place on the ideological and social level but also the political level and—in strictly limited cases—the military.[4]

(b) This political love is the fundamental material of political holiness. But the practice of political love offers a structural cause favourable to specific virtues which are more difficult to attain in other courses. It favours a specific form of ascesis which goes back to fundamental Christian ascesis: *kenosis*, going down into the world of poverty and the poor, a stripping of self; the ascesis necessary in order to denounce and unmask oppression, to have historical patience and solidarity with the poor. It favours the growth of a mature faith and hope in a situation where they will be tried to the utmost. It favours Christian creativity (pastoral, liturgical, theological, spiritual) generated from the underside of history.

It also leads, almost *ex opere operato* to persecution. This is the inexorable fulfilment of Jesus' preaching. Political love, unlike other forms of love, unleashes the specific suffering of persecution by all the powers of this world. Not all Christians, but political Christians are attacked, vilified, threatened, expelled, arrested, tortured and murdered.

This persecution proves that there has been a love which is fundamental; remaining in it means an outstanding exercise of Christian fortitude and a notable witness to faith. If persecution leads to the sacrifice of our own life, if in this sacrifice there is love for the poor majority which was the beginning of the whole process of political love, then the sacrifice of our life becomes martyrdom. This bears witness to the greatest love for the poor and also bears witness objectively to the God of life. Our death is for the cause of justice, but either explicitly or anonymously, for the cause of God's justice. That is why we speak of martyrdom. Of course it is a different matter whether each and every one of those who have fallen or been assassinated for political causes were perfect in all the orders of Christian life. But we cannot deny the great and fundamental love with which they gave their lives. As Mons. Romero said about a murdered priest: 'For me they are truly martyrs in the popular sense. They are men who went all the way in their preaching of solidarity with poverty. They are real men who went to the most dangerous limits to say what they wanted to tell someone and they ended up being killed as Christ was killed' (23.9.1979).[5]

The large numbers of these deaths is what not only enables us to speak *a priori* of the possibility of political holiness, but what forces us to speak of it *a posteriori*. If the spilt blood of so many bishops, priests, nuns, catechists, teachers, and also of Christians who are peasants, workers, trade unionists and fighters, is not a convincing argument that the political is a proper sphere for holiness and moreover that at the moment holiness normally means involvement with politics, then there is no theological discourse which could convince.[6]

But anyone who is not convinced, at least by some clear cases, would be unable to interpret Jesus' death as the death of the Just One either. He would be left with the alternative of interpreting it as the death of a blasphemer and subversive person, as the powers of his time wanted.

(c) This political holiness is what bears witness structurally today to God's holiness in its incarnate form. God is the holy mystery and as mystery, he is always beyond human beings and history: hence the essence of holiness came to be defined as separation and distance from the profane. But since Jesus this has to be corrected.

God who is a holy mystery has come close to us: he has broken the symmetry of being either salvation or condemnation. And this nearness is doubly scandalous: it is a nearness of the mystery of God and a *special* nearness to the poor and oppressed. Because he loves them (Puebla n. 1142), God has come out on their side, fights against the idols of death and shows himself clearly as the God of justice who truly wants the life of the poor. And since Jesus, this is the new and scandalous holiness of God: coming close to the poor to save them and sharing their lot on the cross of Jesus.

This is what the *political* saint or holy person is saying today. He is doing no more that repeat God's action in approaching the poor majorities for the sake of their liberation and assuming the destiny of this nearness. This is the final theological reason why political holiness is a possibility and historically a necessity. There is no other way of telling the world today that God truly loves the poor majority.

3. POLITICS THAT REQUIRE HOLINESS

'I believe, brothers, that the saints were the most ambitious people. This is my ambition for all of you and for myself: that we may be great, ambitiously great, because we are images of God and we cannot be content with mediocre greatness' (Mons. Romero 23.9.1979).

(*a*) The area of politics is necessary for holiness: but it remains a created area. This means it is a limited area, it has its own special temptations and tends to have its own special sins because, especially because, it is about the use of power.

There are historical—not necessarily ethical—limitations involved in the poor keeping in proper perspective the simultaneity of revolution and reconciliation, justice and freedom, new structures and new people, the messianic ideal and the reality that mitigates it. There also exists *at* the ethical level, the concupiscence active in those who practise political action even with the intentions we described above. By its very nature political action may tempt us, to a greater or lesser degree, to exchange the liberation of the poor for the triumph of what we have converted into our own personal or collective cause, the pain of the poor for the passion that politics generates, service for hegemony, truth for propaganda, humility for dominance, gratitude for moral superiority. There is the danger of making absolute the sphere of reality in which the struggle for—social, political or military—liberation takes place and thus abandoning other important spheres of reality—also the reality of poor people—which sooner or later will avenge themselves on this absoluteness. Finally there is the difficulty of keeping up the political love described above to its ultimate consequences because of the conflicts and risks that go with it.

This limitation and concupiscence of the political sphere in no way invalidates the need for it to be the sphere for holiness. Other spheres too (personal ascesis, prayer, the practice of charity)—and this is too often forgotten—are limited and have their own temptations. But these dangers show the need to engage in politics in the right spirit, so that political love may be and remain *love* and liberating political projects should always remain open to the kingdom of God.

(*b*) We see this necessity today, but not just—although also—because human beings need spirit by the mere fact that they *are* spiritual and need it in every area of their lives, but also because Christians who most fully practise political love demand it.

We need the spirit of Jesus in political action too and in those areas that have most to do with politics. We need purity of heart to see the truth of things, to analyse genuinely successes and failures in struggles and plans for liberation, to keep as a criterion for action what will most benefit the poor majorities, to overcome the temptation to dogmatism, to which it is so easy to succumb in all political activity. We need to seek peace even in the midst of the necessary struggle without turning violence, even when it is just and legitimate, into a kind of mysticism, and without placing all our confidence in it to resolve objective problems and neglecting other more peaceful forms of struggle both before and during the armed struggle. We need pity so that we do not relativise disproportionately the people's pain and reduce it to a necessary social cost, so that we do not close off the future from the enemy, so that we do not suppress the difficult possibility of forgiveness and reconciliation. We need the humility to know that fundamentally we are 'unprofitable servants', sinners, so that in action we remain grateful, in difficulty we ask for help and we do the work of liberation as forgiven sinners.

(c) This spirit is the holiness which political action demands if it is to remain and grow in love. Attaining it is personally difficult and structurally Utopian. But this does not mean that this holiness is idealist. On the contrary it is historically effective.

This holiness in the political is what today bears witness to the holiness of God in his eschatological formality. The God come close of whom we spoke of earlier is also the God who transcends history not as a pure Being beyond but as a Utopian Principle. As Utopian his reality is never adequately realisable, but as a principle he rules over historical realities. This does not mean that the eschatological reserve makes all historical realities and all political action relative, but it is the touchstone of history and political action always has a north towards which it should direct itself.

The person with political holiness is one who always keeps in view the ideal of the kingdom of God and the God of the kingdom with which to conform history and his own practice. In spite of his difficulties he always maintains the primacy of life, justice, the necessary struggle, the necessary revolutions and structural reforms but also maintains the necessity for life to be made full, for truth and freedom, reconciliation and change of heart. He also maintains the even more difficult simultaneity of both types of ideal.

This holiness is repeating in history God's action which is eschatologically holy. It is necessary for the Christian to maintain his specificity in political action, but also for him to be more effective and succumb less easily to his temptations. In the short term this holiness may seem like a hindrance because it dedicates energies to what it not purely political action. It may appear idealist because of its intrinsic difficulty. But in the long run it is also fruitful historically, as Mons. Romero demonstrated in an exemplary manner.[7] By his word and example he introduced spirit into the reality and the struggle of the Salvadorean people; by this spirit he made the people more firmly committed to their liberation, more politically effective and more awake to any turning aside of political action which did not take the good of the poor majority with absolute seriousness.

4. NECESSITY AND IMPORTANCE OF POLITICAL HOLINESS

Political saints are a reality. Suffering peoples recognise as saints those who embody themselves through love in the political and they only recognise as saints of today those who take the risks of this incarnation.

This may be done in different ways and the sacrifice of their lives is their ultimate justification. Some examples are the pastoral work of the four US missionaries, Maura, Ita, Jean and Kathy, the ministerial work of Mons. Romero or the explicitly revolutionary engagement of Gaspar Garcia Laiana. At the moment we also need to speak not only of individual saints but collectives of the poor, whole peoples who share in political holiness when they fight for the liberation of the poor, filling these struggles with Christian spirit, and share in the fate of the servant of Jahweh by their very condition as a crucified people.

There are of course various degrees of this holiness. It does not tend to coincide with what the Church still means by holiness in the processes of canonisation. In the end only God knows the measure of real love in these new saints. But none of this should lead us to ignore this new, surprising and massive fact or fail to see its full importance. Political holiness is historically necessary today for the poor to receive the good news and for history to move towards the coming of God's kingdom. It is also important for the

Church itself, so that within it may recover the truth of the Gospel and make this the foundation of its mission, and so that externally it may retain its credibility which it can only keep among humankind today if it offers effective love to the poor. Only thus will it be able to face the challenge to the future of the faith when other struggles for the salvation of the poor are undertaken by those who do not accept the God of Jesus Christ.

It is difficult to maintain political holiness in the two aspects we mentioned, and maintain it in both simultaneously. But now it is a necessity and it is not at all falsely spiritual to call it a gift of God. This is how Mons. Romero saw it. Far better than a long analysis, some of his words explain what is political holiness, how to find it and how to be grateful for it:

'Brothers, I rejoice that our Church is persecuted because it has chosen the poor and because it has tried to become incarnate with the poor' (15.7.1979).

'It would be sad if, in a country where there are so many horrible assassinations, there were not some priests among the victims. They are the witness of the Church incarnate in the problems of the people' (24.6.1979).

Translated by Dinah Livingstone

Notes

1. On the general subject of this article, see L. Boff *La fe en la periferia del mundo* (Santander 1981) pp. 209-262; the monographic issue on 'Spirituality of Liberation' in *Christus* 529 (Mexico 1979-80).

2. Mons. Romero developed his thinking on this point in 'La dimension política de la fe desde la opción por los pobres' published in J. Sobrino, I. Martin-Baro, R. Cardenal *La voz de los sin voz* (San Salvador 1980) pp. 163-183.

3. See I. Ellacuría 'Los pobres, lugar teológico en América Latina' *Diakonia* 21 (Managua 1982) 41-57.

4. See Mons. Romero's pastoral letters in *La voz de los sin voz* pp. 93-172; for his treatment of violence, see *ibid.* pp. 113-119, 156-159, 435-445.

5. See Juan Hernandez Pico 'Martyrdom Today in Latin America: Stumbling-block, Folly and Power of God' in this same issue of *Concilium*; J. Sobrino *Resurrección de la verdadera Iglesia* (Santander 1981) pp. 177-209, 243-266; 'Persecución a la Iglesia en Centroamerica' *Estudios Centroamericanos ECA* 393 (San Salvador 1981) 645-664.

6. On the problem of fighters as possible martyrs, see Juan Hernandez Pico in the article cited in note 5; J. Sobrino *Resurrección de la verdadera Iglesia* p. 197 ff.

7. See I. Ellacuría 'El verdadero pueblo de Dios según Mons. Romero' *ECA* 392 (1981) 529-554.

Francisco Claver

Persecution of Christians by Christians and the Unity of the Church

Prenote. The style of this article is not impersonal, detached, objective—as a scholarly disquisition fitting this journal should be. The first person, singular and plural, is used throughout. The subject is something that touches us very deeply and it would be rather artificial trying for a more 'objective' manner of treatment.   F.C.

OUR PROBLEM. Living under a dictatorship, especially under a 'benign' one as ours claims to be, presents no problem to us as a Church—so long as we are willing to close our eyes to the evils it creates in the lives of our people. Some of us do, some of us do not, and still others try doing neither or both. And we are accordingly persecuted or favoured or ignored by the regime. The persecuting, favouring, ignoring, and, even prior to these, the option or non-option for blindness or sight—these do not make for unity in the Church. The statement sounds condescending—as if *we* had sight, others did not. Not so. The problem is one of perspective—*what* perspective to choose or not choose and what to do or not do about it.

The problem is an old one. It has been with us in the Philippines for all the years we have lived under one-man rule and before.[1] And it will be a constant problem, and a divisive one too—we see this only too clearly—as long as there is no common understanding of what the Church's task is in the area of politics, as long as there is no common approach *from the Gospel* for us *as Church*. The underlined phrases are, I believe, of key importance to any attempt at arriving at some viable solution to the problem we are dealing with here.

PAPAL COUNSEL. In February last year, on the occasion of his visit to the Philippines, Pope John Paul II had some words of advice for the Philippine Church as a whole on precisely this problem. He repeated what he had said at Puebla to the bishops of Latin America:

> You are the priests and religious; you are not social or political leaders or officials of a temporal power. . . . Let us not be under the illusion that we are serving the Gospel if we 'dilute' our charism through an exaggerated interest in the wide field of temporal problems.[2]

As in Latin America, so in the Philippines, these words were immediately picked up and used by the *enemies of the Church*—the term is here deliberately chosen—to warn priests and religious, other Church people, against 'interference' in political questions. Within the Church itself, conservative bishops took up the warning in pretty much the same sense as the government-controlled media did to admonish against social and political 'activism' within the Church.

We fully agree with the holy father: Priests, religious, bishops too, are not political leaders or officials of a temporal power (we exempt, of course, papal nuncios as functionaries, the pope himself as head, of the Vatican State). But we also fully agree with the Holy Father, as he constantly exhorted the Philippine Church in other talks of his during the visit, that we must be deeply concerned about the poor, about their bad political and economic condition. This double agreement is easily and simply made, but yet beneath and beyond that ease and simplicity, in the agreement itself, is buried a can of worms: the complex problem of our political involvement and action *as* Church.

COMPLEXITIES. We rephrase the problem in all its contradictions thus: (1) We are not political leaders or officials of a temporal power—but we have to be totally immersed in the temporal order, work for its transformation unto the kingdom of Christ. (2) We are, in our seeking of the kingdom, essentially and primarily men and women of the spirit—but doing something about the broken lives of the least of Christ's brethren, their suffering, their injustices, their unfreedoms, is pre-eminently a Gospel task that is intimately bound up with the kingdom. (3) We may not dilute our charism and the Church's mission 'through an exaggerated interest' in temporal problems—but interest we must have from the general mandate of charity, be concerned as Christ was concerned with anything that makes people suffer needlessly. (4) Our interest may not be exaggerated, simplistic, obsessive—but when temporal problems are such as to destroy people's humanity and faith itself, our interest must be intense and all-pervading, undeterred and undaunted by the power and violence of those who can kill.

The question to my mind is not that clerics and religious are not political leaders, nor that we dilute our charism and delude ourselves, nor that we go to extremes in our interest in temporal affairs. These are problems, to be sure, but beyond all of these, the prior and more fundamental question is: What is the Gospel way—there is such a thing—of involving ourselves precisely in temporal problems, especially when these, because of their enormity, dehumanise, destroy, kill? What perspective does the Gospel demand of us in the Christian task of renewing the face of the earth? How do we renew *all* things in Christ?

OUR APPROACH. Asking the question is not by any means a speculative, academic exercise. At least not to us here in the Philippines, and, I suspect, to many a Church in Latin America and most of the Third World where poverty and injustice are ordinary conditions of life of the people *and* the Church with the people seeks to do something about those same conditions. Thus, here in the Philippines, development—economic, that is—is the obsession of the day for the government. We will not delay on the specificities of the kind of development it is pursuing. Suffice it to say that it is extremely capitalistic and western in concept, dependent on exploitive foreign industries for its execution, and fully backed by the machinery of a 'national security' State for its continuance. The economic and political interests of the powerful few are fused into one controlling systemic order. The net effect is an excess of poverty and pauperisation for the many—and their institutionalised enslavement. Exaggerated? I suggest that people who say so try living as our people do.

So we, as Church, try doing something with our people about the many evils of their life situation. In the trying, we have to look into the causes of these evils, analyse them,

C

see where their roots lie. We have to ask questions about the model of society current development programmes are based on. We have to face up too to such alternative models as are being presented to our people by various political groups. We have to consider closely the whole problematic of ideologies, approaches to, methods and strategies of social change and restructuring. And above all, we have to clarify for ourselves what our own Christian vision of the kingdom is.

We have to do all this in prayerful discernment, ever groping, ever seeking to learn where the Spirit leads and what the faith demands we should do. The discerning, seeking, doing—these we attempt not in aseptic, ivory-tower conditions but in the midst of hunger, want, oppression, violence. These we do where people are being forced to choose between alternatives that—to us at least—are no alternatives at all: between the totalitarianism of the right or that of the left, between the guns of the soldiers of the regime or those of insurgents fighting the regime, between murder by the military (on the grounds of our being subversive) or by the NPA[3] (on the grounds of our hindering *the* revolution).

Under these conditions, the pope's warning against our involvement in politics gains deeper meaning—or, the exact contrary, loses all meaning.

We prefer to see a deeper meaning in the pope's words. Not because we want to allay the fears and suspicions of curial Rome about our 'excessive socio-political orientation' but simply because we find no other meaning to what we are doing than what, we believe, the pope is trying to tell us.

PROPHECY AND COMPROMISE. But what is the pope telling us? Two things, to my mind: (1) that the Church must preach the message of the Gospel in its fullness; and (2) that in its preaching, it may not subordinate the Gospel to political expediences. These two ideas, I believe, cut through to the core of the problem we started out with, divergent though our reading may be here in the Philippines of his words and acts during his visit to us last year, divergent though our approaches are to the whole question of our competence as Church in matters political.

If the Church is to preach the Gospel in its fullness, not selectively, not partially, there are no two ways about it, it will have to be totally prophetic in such a situation as we have in the Philippines. Anything less would be a dilution and a denial of its mission to bring the saving Word into the life of people. And if it plays its prophetic role faithfully, there is no question about it, it will be involved in politics (however the word is defined). Thus I cannot see how, for instance, we can denounce the violence of Communists but not that of the regime, even in the supposition that the latter is the lesser evil; or vice versa, denounce the violence of the government but not that of Communists—on the grounds that criticism of Communists at this time blocks the momentum of the revolution, the 'last resort' for our heavily oppressed people. Hence, the substantive question in the Church's involvement in politics does not seem to be so much the *what* as the *how* of it.

This, I believe, is the second point the pope was making: When he warned priests and religious against taking part in politics, I cannot understand his admonition except in this sense, that in our work to bring about a better world, to transform it, to effect more justice, we may not subordinate the demands of the Gospel to the exigencies of personal and party politics. The perspectives of the Gospel and it values must guide us in whatever we do in the political sphere—as in all other aspects of life; the power that we have in our faith must be used to build up, never to destroy, people.

THE POWER OF THE CHURCH. The power mentioned above can bear a little more scrutiny. For from a sheerly human point of view, the ultimate reason for the persecution of Christians—to bring our discussion back to the subject of this paper—may be the simple fact that they have power.

The power we speak of here is not the power of jurisdiction that matters so much to canonists and ecclesiastics, the power to govern the faithful. Nor do we speak, at least not directly, of the power the Church has in its sacramental ministry, the power to sanctify and bless. We speak rather of the power that comes from the doing of the faith and the witnessing to the justifying love of Christ, the power to proclaim and do the truth that makes men free. It is the 'spiritual' power that the holy father seemed to have had in mind when he declared that clerics and religious are not officials of a temporal power.

We can give this power any name we wish—holiness, soul-force, moral influence, integrity of the spirit, spiritual power—but by whatever name we may call it, however we understand and define it, in the simple fact that it does change minds and hearts towards the values of the kingdom, impel people to live and work according to these values, it does have much to do with affairs of the temporal order. Hence, how we as Church are to use it in that same order, this is the constant problem. For if in our proclaiming of the Gospel we deal not with timeless, disembodied souls but with people of the flesh-and-blood present, then we have to use the power of the Gospel to help them to live the faith as fully as possible in this imperfect and perfectible world, through it transforming this world unto the kingdom in the very living.

The problematic of the Church's involvement in politics and, more generally, in the temporary order, does seem to revolve around the question of how it uses this power. In the Philippines, to bring the question down to concrete reality, we have churchmen who see nothing wrong with working with the government of President Marcos: they believe he is the only viable deterrent to a Communist take-over; Communism is condemned by the Church, *ergo*. . . . We have other Church people, on the contrary, who see nothing wrong either with working for a Communist revolution: they believe the capitalistic structure of Philippine society is evil and must be replaced by a more egalitarian Communist state. There are other forces, other powers or would-be powers at work, and in the conflicting visions and allegiances that they demand of their supporters, we are compelled to seek a clearer understanding of the Church's proper power and its uses for the building up of the kingdom.

Thus, in all the political manoeuverings going on around us, within and without the Church, we are no longer bothered overmuch by the charge of political meddling: we see only too well that even what traditional churchmen define as the Church's spiritual power has deep implications for the political order. We are not bothered either by the fact that priests and religious do engage in *real* politics in the strictest sense of the word: as private citizens they are entitled to a political ideology of their choosing.[4] Nor, finally, are we troubled by the disunity in the Church that results from the two above-mentioned facts: political options will vary even among the holiest of men and debating the differences in these options is often like arguing about tastes.

But we are deeply troubled by one thing: the use of the Church's power for ends not always in keeping with the Gospel and by means foreign to that same Gospel. We cannot put it any other way. Nor as simply. Hence our continuing concern—as we put it in the beginning of this paper—with our *perspectives as Church*, and with perspectives that are formed in and by *the Gospel*.

UNITY. When all the distinctions and sub-distinctions are made about the Church's political involvement—and here it does not make one bit of a difference whether we speak of clerical or lay participation (our structures apply to both) or whether the Church's 'spiritual' power is in fact political in every sense of the word or not—we come to only one conclusion: If the Christian is to involve himself in politics, *he must do so as a Christian*. It sounds like the most sterile of formulas. And most simplistic. It probably is. But to Christians whose faith is put to the test daily by all kinds of outrages and inhumanities visited on the weak by the powerful for the sake of *their* power, it is heavy with meaning, very heavy. For it means we have to work mightily at all times for justice without ourselves becoming unjust. We have to strive to lessen the ills of poverty—to bring about economic development, yes—without ourselves turning materialistic and selfish. We have to struggle along with the powerless for their rightful empowering without ourselves becoming manipulative, power-mad, ruthless. All this and more is meant by being Christians in the politics of our day here in the Philippines.

It is bad politics, we are told by the more politically sophisticated. But we know it is good Christianity. If it were not, we might as well forget Christ and adore Caesar. And because we do not, because we seek to tell Caesar there are other things in life more important than, or at least as important as, physical well-being and comfort, power and domination, we come under persecution—by Christians.

In some mysterious way, the disunity among us Christians that we noted earlier will not happen or will not be so polarising in its effects if we all seek to take seriously the Church's prophetic role in and out of politics and to be open to the persecution that will inevitably come from our faithful and faith-filled playing of that role.

Our deepest unity as Christians is in our striving to live the Paschal Mystery in its fullness. The enemies of the Church seem to be more aware of this fact than we are. If this is so, then, we must *see*.

Notes

1. 'Martial Law' was imposed by President Marcos on 21 Sept. 1972. It was lifted on 19 Jan. 1980, four weeks before the pope's visit in February of that same year. The name 'Martial Law' was taken away, the fact remains.

2. *Acta Apostolicae Sedis* 71 (1979), p. 193.

3. The New People's Army, the armed portion of the Communist (Maoist) Party of the Philippines.

4. As a Prelature, we have deliberately opted for non-alignment with any political group. We—bishop, priests, religious, lay leaders—are only too conscious of the fact that the Official Church is more credible in its prophetic task without such alignments.

PART II

Profiles of Contemporary Martyrdom

Enda McDonagh

Dying for the Cause:
An Irish Perspective on Martyrdom

1. THE IRISH POLITICAL TRADITION

IN THE wake of the London bombings of 20 July 1982, in which ten soldiers died, responsible British politicians rejected the suggestion that the death penalty should be introduced for terrorists, partly on the grounds that it would provide the IRA with fresh 'martyrs'. The IRA hunger-strikers who died in 1981 were regarded by their followers and some outside observers as such political martyrs, dying to bear witness to the justice of their political cause. (I had this confirmed in discussion with Africans from South Africa in August 1982.) In all this supporters and opponents of the present IRA campaign are very conscious of the explicit invocation of martyrdom with all its sacred overtones by the Irish political tradition to which the IRA proclaims allegiance. The Manchester 'martyrs' executed by the British in 1867 were a paradigm case. In the run-up to the next revolution in Easter 1916 the leaders set great store by the Fenian dead and their graves, like the early Christians honouring the martyrs and their tombs. Padraic Pearse, ultimately commander-in-chief of the revolutionary forces, spoke of the need for bloody self-sacrifice by the few to restore the self-respect and the spirit of Ireland. The execution of the 1916 leaders shortly after the collapse of the revolution did indeed reawaken the Irish drive for independence. The name and role of martyr continued to fuel that struggle for independence.

Some later commentators have expressed shock at the appropriation by a secular political cause (Irish Nationalism) of the properly religious tradition of martyrdom and at the consequent confusion between nationalism and religion. The confusion has been compounded in Ireland (as elsewhere) by the close (but not entire) overlapping between religious and political traditions. In Ireland Nationalists, favouring Irish independence from Britain, have been mainly but not exclusively Catholic; Unionists, in favour of maintaining the union with Britain, have been dominantly Protestant. The martyrs and saints of the one side tend to be the enemies and demon-figures of the other; William of Orange and Sir Edward Carson on the Unionist side v. Wolfe Tone (Protestant) and Padraic Pearse on the Nationalist side.

Ireland is by no means unique in honouring political martyrs with a religious intensity, as it is not alone in the near coincidence of opposing political and religious traditions. Ireland's tangled history and the continuing destructive instability of Northern Ireland demand careful reflection on the meaning and role of martyrdom as it emerged in Christian tradition, and developed in the history of the West. How far it already contained or subsequently acquired a political dimension; whether and when this political dimension became a dominant one; how far martyrdom entered into a people's self-definition or identity; and whether this identity, religious or political, became a closed and excluding identity issuing in idolatry: these are questions which a contemporary study of martyrdom must face. They are questions which the particular case-study of Ireland can partially illuminate, if not finally answer.

2. MARTYRS IN THE CHRISTIAN TRADITION: RELIGIOUS OR POLITICAL?

The early Christian martyrs who shaped Christian praxis and theory of martyrdom, were consciously witnessing to Jesus Christ, to his Gospel, his person and his achievement. They saw themselves as followers and imitators willing to 'confess him before men', taking up their cross to follow him, following and imitating him even unto his death on a cross. His laying down of his life for his friends was their model and inspiration. His conflict with and execution by the religious and political establishment of his day was accepted as their inevitable lot. They attempted to maintain continuity with Israel in temple and synagogue. Their proto-martyr Stephen and the presence at his death of arch-persecutor Saul exposed the deepening rift. More significant in space and time was the presence and power of the Empire to which they persistently proclaimed allegiance. It was a necessarily qualified allegiance to a necessarily relativised Empire. The kingdom which Jesus had preached and to which Christians must be primarily loyal, was not indeed of this world in the sense of its being a historical, political alternative to the Empire or the other kingdoms of this world. Yet its proclamation and the allegiance it demanded relativise all human kingdoms. Membership of them could not exhaust the reality of citizens who were called to recognise the presence and power of the saving God of Jesus Christ in the incoming kingdom which he had announced and inaugurated. A historical kingdom which absolutised itself, which required worship of its gods as well as obedience to its laws, as the Roman Empire did, conflicted with the claim of one true God and his kingdom. Christians realised that they had to obey God rather than men and their created deities or idols. The Roman Empire like all political kingdoms would now be relativised, radically diminished. To that threat the Empire reacted defensively violently in persecution of the Christians. Christian martyrs died bearing witness to the power and presence of God which Jesus embodied in himself and proclaimed as the kingdom.

Without entering into the details of the debate of how far and in what way the mission and death of Jesus were precisely political for that time and place, one can say that his mission and death had the undeniable political effect of relativising and restraining all historical political enterprises. They might no longer make the absolute and divine claims advanced by the Roman Empire and repeated in frequently harsher terms by absolute or totalitarian regimes ever since. In maintaining and defending unto death this freedom to recognise and respond to their God, the early Christians opened up a permanent area of freedom for the person and revealed a permanent limitation of politics and the law. In this area of freedom and by recognition of this limitation of politics, the person is seen to transcend the citizen and what we now call human rights to transcend political authority and State law. This is a critical and in principle irreversible political achievement initiated by Christianity and its early martyrs.

The achievement in principle was frequently obscured in practice once Christianity became part of the imperial establishment. This is illustrated by the switch in Augustine's attitude to the Donatists from commitment to persuasion and free conversion to invoking the aid of the Roman council and appealing to the Scriptural text

'Compel them to come in'. The history of Christendom renders at best ambiguous evidence to the limitations on the political and to the freedom of the person to which the early martyrs bore witness. The death of Thomas à Becket, Archbishop of Canterbury, at the hands of Henry II shows how Christian witness survived in face of political claims. Too many episcopal colleagues of Becket, from Rome to Canterbury, were more ready to collaborate with and even encourage political rulers in activities that reflected absolute rather than relative claims over their subjects. This they demonstrated in conversion by the sword and in the execution of heretics as traitors. Such practices persisted long after the break-up of Christendom both in the new world and in the post-Reformation States. As the modern world was born, Christians, now belonging to different and opposing churches, were long in disrepute as the defenders of persons against powers, as upholders of freedom, even religious freedom, except for the narrow confines of their own denominational members. The potential for personal freedom and restraint on power which Christian martyrdom had expressed, was for the most part obscured by alliance with power in pursuit of Church privilege. The new champions of freedom were avowedly secular in origin and aim. Such champions included witness unto death for the new secular and political freedom heralded for example by the American and French revolutions.

In its dependent and oppressed tradition Ireland was influenced by the new freedom involvements. Theobald Wolfe Tone, father of Irish republicanism, was greatly influenced by Paine's *The Rights of Man* and strenuously sought to enlist the aid of the new French revolutionary government. The 1798 Irish revolution, despite its failure and that of the French expedition, and despite the death of Wolfe Tone in prison, initiated a new stage in the struggle for civil and political freedoms by oppressed Irish Catholics and in the more radical movement for separation from England into an independent republic.

It is from the inevitable convergence of these two struggles for Catholic Emancipation and political independence that the present-day intertwining of Catholicism and Nationalism stems. It is from the more radical separatist republican tradition that the latter-day Irish political 'martyrs' have come. Have the secularising and relativising of politics by the early Christian martyrs given way to the resacralising and absolutising of them by the new political martyrs from Ireland and a host of other countries? Or is there a Christian sense to secular and political martyrdom of the kind experienced in Ireland?

3. MARTYRDOM AND IDENTITY: QUESTIONS AND AMBIGUITIES

In the course of history Christian martyrs have presented the Church with opportunities and demands to identity itself as the community witnessing to the saving presence and power of God in the world, the kingdom announced by and inaugurated in Jesus Christ. The need for such self-identification by the Church continues. The need for witnesses, even unto death, to question and relativise the powers of this world is no less real although the manner of doing so varies enormously. Unless the Church in its witness is questioning and exposing the absolute pretensions of political, economic and other contemporary powers, Jesus' kingdom will continue to be obscured and obstructed. Where that witness is finally death-accepting in the cause, after the fashion and by the power of Jesus, the life-giving proclamation of the Gospel is renewed. Maximilian Kolbe, Dietrich Bonhoeffer, Martin Luther King and Archbishop Romero encourage the hope of renewal for the current generations.

Yet historical and contemporary martyrdom raise a number of serious questions about the causes for which 'martyrs' die, the manner in which they meet their death and the effects which their deaths have on the communities to which they belong. Despite the apparently clear and clean historical record of the people we honour as Christian martyrs, ambiguities abound.

4. THE CAUSE

In so many ways in the history and theology of Christian martyrdom the cause has been crucial. This corresponds to the wider Christian tradition on life and death issues in which the 'just cause' in the case of war provides a characteristic example. The general point at issue here is the critical role of 'cause' in understanding and evaluating life and death issues for the Christian.

The identifying of the martyr's cause as Jesus' cause and the translation of that into witness to the kingdom does not remove all the obscurities and ambiguities as the different circumstances and causes of Justin Martyr and Maximilian Kolbe Martyr or the 'opposing' causes of Catholic and Protestant martyrs at the time of the Reformation readily reveal. An important continuity of cause recur, I believe, and may be expressed as witness to God's kingdom even when that takes on more apparently secular form in service and protection of the neighbour. Jesus ultimately witnessing to the kingdom was Jesus laying down his life for his friends. Despite the obvious connection between Church community and kingdom of God, Christian martyrs do not die solely even primarily for the sake of the Church community but for the kingdom which may be seeking expression and demanding recognition within the bounds of the historical Church, in causes not explicitly religious. So much the centrality of love of neighbour to the appearance and practice of the kingdom should always tell us.

The broader reaches of love of neighbour clearly provide adequate cause for giving one's life. In the many oppressive situations in which one lives today that life-giving will have an immediately political rather than religious context as, in their different ways, Kolbe, Bonhoeffer, King and Romero discovered. Their and others' recognition as Christian martyrs, as witnesses unto death to the truth and grace of God's kingdom, will reflect their own and the Christian community's understanding of their enterprise, dying for their friends in the manner and by the power of Jesus Christ.

It would be foolish to resist extending the range of Christian martyrdom then to those who give their lives for their neighbour in political contexts. It would be equally foolish to interpret all deaths for political causes as unambiguous instances of Christian martyrdom.

The understanding of the people themselves and of the Christian community is relevant to the recognition of martyrs, but the prior more objective criterion of the cause as some inbreaking of the kingdom is not always easily applicable. The opposing political options for Northern Ireland illustrate the difficulty of identifying political causes as Christian causes to which one might bear witness with one's life. There is, however, some further guidance available on the appropriateness of the cause as one reflects on its effects, particularly the relationship between martyrdom and identification

The self-identification of a community by its appeal to its 'martyrs' does not apply exclusively to religious communities. The invocation of Fenian graves by leaders of the Irish revolution has already been quoted as a political instance. The Irish conflict clearly involves a conflict of identities nurtured by the memory of martyrs in conflict.

A critical Christian question for such community identification and its martyr support, is how far a fresh human absolute has emerged. How far, in the Irish instance, is the supreme determinant of allegiance and behaviour membership of a United Ireland or of the United Kingdom? Does some national political ideal override all other consideration, including considerations of life and death? Has the ideal become an idol to which we surrender all that we are and have, including our sense of the relativity of all such ideals in the face of God's kingdom? Have we found a substitute God, an alternative supreme being, more properly described in that telling term as a godling? A test of where our final allegiance lies will continue to be, what are we prepared to die for? A more frightening one may be, what are we prepared to kill for? And pressing that test further we ask how far the ideal is pursued at the expense of the people? How far the what has replaced the who in the evaluation of our killing and dying?

This is not intended as a complete evaluation of killing or dying for political causes. It is calling attention to how these causes may be absolutised and how that absolutising involves the relativising of people, even whole races or generations as we have experienced in this century. Such absolutising is the antithesis rather than the expression of the kingdom and dying for it does not fit the pattern of Christian martyrdom.

Political leaders are not the only people exposed to the temptations of absolutising. Political ideals and the power centred about them are not the only ones which take on the mantle of idol. Church leaders and Church power may yield to the same temptations. And killing in the name of Church or Jesus as evidenced in the Crusades and frequently invoked to bless subsequent wars, offers an important clue to the failure of the Church to see itself as limited embodiment and servant of the kingdom but not identical with it.

All this may not be taken as an excuse to ignore the justice and urgency of particular causes or the obligation to enter the struggle for them as deriving from our kingdom commitment. Indeed it may not be taken to exclude the need to fight for them by means of physical force in particular circumstances. It does, however, call attention to the ambiguities of such causes, the dangers that they may easily be absolutised, how this danger may be enhanced by the appeal to martyrs and how this absolutising easily leads to killing rather than dying for one's cause. One should be very circumspect therefore in using the name 'martyr', restricting it as far as possible to where somebody clearly sacrificed him or herself to maintain or achieve justice for others, a clearly kingdom cause.

5. VICTIMS AND MARTYRS

The others constitute the primary test of all genuine self-sacrifice, the others in their needs, in their privations and oppressions, the others as victims. Victimhood and martyrdom are intimately connected. All martyrs are victims, victims of human powers pretending to be absoluteness. But are all victims martyrs? Are all the millions of victims of historical powers we have known even in this century to be classified as martyrs, dying for the kingdom, however implicitly? Perhaps many more are than we have previously recognised, their witness lost on us. Yet some distinction between martyr and victim may be necessary to preserve the traditional force of martyrdom without letting us lapse once again into the forgetfulness of the victims which remains such a disturbing feature of human consciousness, including that of Christians.

The witness of Jesus was expressed in his victimhood. The victim of Calvary, on one important reading, was carrying to its conclusion his identification of himself and his God with the victims of the society in which he lived. By siding with them, attending to them, identifying with them he took on their victimhood, he accepted human victimhood itself. That acceptance and its expression on Calvary may be understood as the victimhood to end all victimhood as it was the sacrifice to end all sacrifices. In Jesus' death and resurrection victimhood was taken on fully and finally overcome. He was the victim to end all victims. The kingdom he proclaimed excluded victimhood. The humble and lowly would be raised from their oppression. The prisoners would be set free.

Victims of physical illness would be healed. The poor, the general category of victims, were to receive this good news (Luke 4). Calvary revealed the last victim as prelude to the new life and freedom, peace and justice of the kingdom.

Yet victimhood goes on. The followers of Jesus are at once puzzled and challenged. Why hasn't the kingdom come? the puzzle. What is our obligation to let it come? the challenge. We must recognise the problems of the puzzle but refuse to be paralysed by it as we take up the challenge—the challenge to remove victimhood, to witness to the coming of the kingdom by opposing and seeking to remove the diverse oppressions which continue to obscure and obstruct the kingdom by creating and maintaining victims. It is in taking on victimhood, by identifying with the victims and struggling for their release that we bear witness to the kingdom. We may do that from a position initially free from the particular condition of the victims, by entering into that condition and seeking to change it. We may seek to do this as victims already enmeshed in that condition and by opposing and seeking to change the conditions, bear witness to and promote the kingdom which excludes victimhood. In opposing the oppressive powers on behalf of the (other) victims we follow Jesus to his bitter end. In giving our lives in such a cause we properly merit the title and honour of martyr, witness unto death to the presence and power of the kingdom.

Martyrs are victims. They share the conditions of victims and by opposing endure the final victimhood of Calvary. They remind Christians of the prevalence and depth of human victimhood and challenge them to oppose in turn. They remind them of the contemporary Calvaries which crowd the world. They seek to live the prayer 'Thy kingdom come' by seeking to remove the victim conditions of the neighbour even at the price of ultimate victimhood.

The coming of the kingdom in history and politics is a summons to Christians. One way to test its concrete demands is to ask who are the victims? One way to make a concrete response is by accepting the cause of the victims. The martyr recognises that response as 'costing not less than everything' (Eliot).

Juan Hernández Pico

Martyrdom Today in Latin America: Stumbling-block, Folly and Power of God

1. A MARTYR CHURCH IN CATHOLIC COUNTRIES AND IN A SECULAR AND TOLERANT WORLD

THE MAIN message which the Church's faith in Jesus Christ is sending today from Latin America is the cry of the blood of its martyrs. It is a controversial message.

Amazement and incredulity were the first reactions to the Latin American martyr Church of today. Firstly, the martyrs were Catholics killed in countries which were culturally Catholic. They thus shattered the schemas according to which the Church undergoes martyrdom in the twentieth century only where atheistic Communism has seized power. Secondly, the martyrs were being killed in countries belonging to the apparently secular and tolerant western civilisation. This was a blow to the confident belief that fanaticism had collapsed in the West after the defeat of Nazi-Fascist irrationality. Finally, in the West Christianity seemed to belong to the respectable order of values, and the churches to the core of powerful institutions. Latin America dislodged the habit of seeing the faith threatened solely by a marginal minority of radical intellectuals and young iconoclasts.

Today this amazement and incredulity no longer exist. There is indignation and admiration, on the part of both non-denominational organisations for the defence of human rights and of international Church circles. Both denounce the political repression which is the context of the deaths of the Latin American martyrs today, and celebrate the martyrs. Nevertheless it is perhaps important to recover that first amazement and incredulity.

The martyrdom of Latin American Catholics created some amazement by revealing that cultural Christianity had been unable to leaven social structures in which there existed 'a situation of social sin', 'a desire for power and domination, for discrimination of all sorts' (Puebla, paras 28, 435, 1300). Martyrdom thus became a denunciation of a predominantly vertical and disincarnate Christianity (see Puebla, 42).

Moreover, since Latin American society is structurally linked with the enrichment and domination of the major western countries, the martyrdom of Catholics in Latin America has also become a denunciation of the hegemonic intransigence of the 'North'

37

and of the victims which post-industrial capitalism claims in Latin America, allegedly in the name of anti-Communism but in fact as part of the accumulation of wealth which it refuses to share (see Puebla, 1209).

The surprise and incredulity were the products of an anachronism. We do not live in the sacralised Roman Empire or in the fourth to the sixth centuries, or at the dawn of capitalism, all periods torn by life-or-death theological disputes. Moreover, the Latin American Church seemed to have agreed not to dictate to the dominant conservative administrations, and so all incentive to persecute it had vanished. However, the surprising persecution and the numerous martyrs have unmasked the idolatrous absolutism intrinsic to transnational Capital's logic of exploitation and domination. This denunciation of radical responsibility for the blood of the martyrs, 'while global, is much more important than a reply giving details of the direct perpetrators of acts of persecution'.[1] From the cry of this blood a new Apocalypse is being written today, one which clearly identifies the 'beast rising out of the sea' (Rev. 13:1) and the 'great harlot . . . sitting at the edge of the ocean' (Rev. 17:1).

This martyrdom contains another crucial message. It consists, not so much in the denunciation as in the hope for the poor proclaimed by the martyrs in their resistance to the idol which capital has become. It is their proclamation of the dawning of the kingdom of God as a gift, and of the value of the struggle for historical approximations to that kingdom.

The historical uniqueness of this witness stands out in the context of legitimate revolution in which persecution and martyrdom take place. It also stands out—in such a context—in the witness of weakness and gratuitousness, as a humanising force in the struggle for justice, in the face of power and heroism. Finally it appears in the difficulty encountered by this martyrdom and persecution in winning recognition in the Church. I shall discuss this uniqueness in the rest of this article.

2. MARTYRDOM WITHIN POLITICAL REVOLUTION FOR JUSTICE

In Latin America today martyrdom is posterior to resistance to injustice and domination. If we take as the starting-point of such resistance, 1910, the year of the Mexican Revolution, we find that its most popular leaders, Zapata and Villa, did not fight in the name of their faith, nor were they backed by the pastors of the Church, though the 'Zapatistas' wore on their hats badges of the Virgin of Guadalupe. Faith and justice were not yet preached in close connection. Nor was there any ecclesial inspiration behind resistance to oppression, not among the Chilean miners in 1907, not in El Salvador in 1932, not in Guatemala in 1954. In fact, the persecution and martyrdom in revolutionary Mexico were ambiguous because they occurred as part of an ill-defined defence of religious freedom and ecclesiastical privileges.

On the other hand, it seems to be a characteristic of ecclesial martyrdom that it originated in a confrontation of Christian faith with power. The first persecutions attacked Christianity as a threat to the Empire's worship. The Protestant and Catholic martyrs of the beginning of the capitalist era also bore witness to the faith by resisting the power of national Christian confessions to impose their will: *cuius regio eius et religio*. No one will be surprised by these and other historical instances, given that Jesus, 'the pioneer and perfecter of our faith' (Heb. 12:2) was executed as an enemy of the State, outside the city (Heb. 13:12).

Nevertheless the Christian resistance to the Roman Empire of which martyrdom was a part did not directly involve opposition to the social system or power structures. Resistance to the point of martyrdom was not focused on slavery or imperial conquests. Its aim was to desacralise power, strongly resisting its pretensions (Rev. 13:8, 14:10-12,

20:4) and fighting for the right to speak and teach about the person of Jesus (Acts 4:18, 5:29-30). The Christians preserved the memory, dangerous for the State, of someone 'excluded from human society' and slandered by an 'impious, unjust and idolatrous world'.[2] The Protestant and Counter-Reformation Catholic martyrs were also defending freedom of conscience, which submits to God alone, as shown with paradigmatic force by Thomas More.[3]

Today in Latin America, too, persecution and martyrdom are coming from a power challenged by the right to speak and teach about the person of Jesus. Now, however, that person is mediated by the crucified of today who question society and its articulation of power. The 'seeds of the Word' discovered in the just revolutionary struggle, the realisation of the compatibility of resistance with following Christ and the Church's preaching against institutionalised violence have stimulated the revolutionary movements of the oppressed.

Incapable of maintaining its power without hating justice, the system has reacted with a persecution translated into psycho-social manifestations of horrible cruelty. Here is the evidence of a Guatemalan Indian Catholic catechist about the practice of the army during its offensive against Chimaltenango in December 1981: 'There was another catechist whom we found with the others. . . . They crucified them alive in the middle of the road, two stakes through the hands, one through the naked stomach another through the bare feet and one through the head. . . .'[4] In March 1976 Colonel Reyes made the following speech to 200 teachers from Quiché: 'If you want to stay alive and not be kidnapped or killed, get out of the Church, as the army has decided to sweep this shit out of Guatemala.'[5]

Bishops, priests, religious and lay people have begun to be persecuted throughout Latin America as agitators and subversives without the need for any anti-religious decrees, just as there was no need to change Jewish or Roman law to execute Jesus, but simply to use it cleverly (see Luke 23:3, 5:14; John 18:30, 19:7, 12).

Ecclesial clarity about the historical uniqueness of this martyrdom is sometimes exemplary. Archbishop Romero formulated it when he said that the Church in this new context did not shed its blood first, but by entering into a commitment to the lives of the poor, 'it has to suffer the same fate as the poor: disappear . . . be tortured . . . captured, be found dead'.[6] In this the Church has broken a model of evangelisation based on denominational or culturally Christian power. Its martyrs, in whom it has rediscovered its crucified God, have in this way become an integral part of the historical scandal of the poor. But the weakness of the cross exemplified in Bishop Angelelli (Argentina), in Luis Espinal (Bolivia), in Frei Tito (Brazil), in Ita, Maura, Kathy and Jean (El Salvador), in the twenty-one priests murdered in Guatemala and El Salvador, in the countless lay people massacred in the struggle for justice, this weakness so visible in the 'hour and the power of darkness' (Luke 22:53),[7] is the power of God. It is 'the voice of justice (which) no one can ever kill',[8] 'the voice of those who have no voice . . . a poor voice (which) will find an echo in those who love truth and truly love our beloved people'.[9]

3. THE WITNESS OF WEAKNESS AND GRATUITOUSNESS IN CONTRAST TO POWER AND HEROISM

Jesus of Nazareth opposed the misrepresentation of God, who had been turned, in the temple of his day, from a God of liberation into a God who oppressed the poor (see John 2:13-22).[10] In this opposition Jesus used elements of violence: whips to drive the dealers from the temple, anger at those who defended the oppressive law (Mark 3:5), and denunciation involving insults (Matt. 23:13-36; Luke 6:24-26, etc.). But he accepted a limit: he ruled out violent resistance to death. In a position more universal and profound than revolutionary zeal, Jesus proclaimed, from his experience of the Father, whose loyalty to the poor went to the point of giving his Son up to oppression and death, that the greater love is shown less ambiguously by the free and patient surrender of one's own life and forgiveness of those who unjustly take it. In this surrender he expressed confidence in victory over death and in the absolute future of justice for persons and for history.

Like Jesus, the Latin American Church accepts in its martyrdom this ultimate failure of resistance in the face of death, not without suffering and anguished prayer, following Jesus in order to be able to sharpen the struggle for life repressed in death: 'My soul is very sorrowful, even to death. Watch and pray that you may not enter into temptation; the spirit indeed is willing, but the flesh is weak' (Mark 14:34, 38).

In this perspective we can face the contrast drawn by Ernst Bloch between the socialist hero and the Christian martyr. The holocaust of the former is 'different from that of the earlier martyrs in that they, almost without exception, died with a prayer on their lips and in the belief that they had won heaven'.[11] The socialist hero, 'in the struggle against the beast of oppression, in the service of the tireless movement of freedom . . . does not seek to be a martyr, but an unyielding fighter'.[12]

Certainly, love nourished in the solidarity of the oppressed can make this grandeur fruitful. On the other hand, the history of many actually existing socialisms reveals another possibility for such 'unyielding' heroism, the subsequent hardening of society, the suppression of millions of human beings, and the sterility, at least partial, of the 'tireless movement of freedom'.

The admitted weakness of the Christian martyrs in Latin America today may come to be a humanising element in this heroism based on commitment and class solidarity. It may be able to show that the humanisation to which the revolutionary movement lays claim is not merely liable to be either obscured 'by inadequacy' or 'bitterly delayed by deviations'.[13] Rather, these political mistakes or errors of calculation, according to the Christian faith of the martyrs, do not have their ultimate root in the ever-perfectible immaturity of the human condition, but in the ever-present possibility of its perversion.

Moreover, the sacrifice of the materialist hero who renounces 'every traditional consolation'[14] depends on revolutionary solidarity enlightened by scientific analysis, which creates a 'humanity which actively understands itself',[15] militantly transforming the world in the direction of the hope contained in its own future. The Christian martyrs, in contrast, in their struggle and its apparently unavoidable failure, retain the consolation that their loving solidarity with the poor is guaranteed by the commitment of God's paternity to the historical hope of the poor.

This testimony in the face of failure also asserts that victory, where it is achieved in history, is God's gift even if it is won by taking control of history through resistance. This historical gratuitousness may help to ensure that class solidarity and the revolutionary future do not turn into 'law' and cease to be 'Gospel'. In the midst of the opacity of history the non-believing revolutionaries of Latin America will be able to aspire to make that history more human through the solidarity in memory which forms the bond between 'the victims of the past and the victors of the future',[16] while they strive to 'humanise nature (as) the ultimate Utopian goal of their praxis'.[17] Meanwhile the Church, including Christian revolutionaries, must continue to recall, in order to humanise history, not only the memory of its martyrs and of all the victims—believers or not—who have fallen in the struggle for justice or who were destroyed in the course of it, but also the memory of Jesus, who was crucified by the unjust and raised up by his Father, the vindicator of his blood and of every injustice.

Gratuitousness, forgiveness and tenderness, not towards exploitation and class oppression, but towards the class enemy and, of course, towards the weakness and inadequacy of comrades, these may be the essential values of the faith to which the martyrs are bearing witness today in Latin America. This faith appears scandalous because it introduces sin into historical rationality, as the rejection of the love of God and the possibility of the destruction of historical aspirations at a level deeper than that of stupidity, triviality or human error. Such a faith is 'folly' because it questions the hope which bases its own venture on the openness of history, on the autonomous 'unfolding of the riches of human nature',[18] and places the anchor of its hope in God.

In the revolutionary conditions of Latin America the witness of the Christian martyrs may be 'the power of God' and not opium if the Church of the martyrs, in the face of oppression and faced with the task of building the future, continues to proclaim with Archbishop Romero: 'It must be made very clear that if what is asked is collaboration in a pseudo-peace, a false order, based on repression and fear, we must remember that the only order and the only peace which God wants are those which are based on truth and justice. In the face of this alternative our choice . . . is clear. We shall obey the command of God rather . . . than the command of human beings.'[19]

4. THE RECOGNITION OF THE LATIN AMERICAN MARTYRS IN THE CHURCH

The final document of the Puebla Conference of Bishops hesitated about the authenticity of the martyrdom of the Church in Latin America today[20]—another unique feature of the present-day martyrs of Latin America compared with other periods.

In Latin America today innocent Christians are being murdered, children still clinging to their mother's breast, adults from the laity, the religious state and the hierarchy. They are also dying in the struggle for justice, like those soldiers of whom St Thomas Aquinas ventured to speculate that they might have been martyrs if they had died 'to defend their country (*rempublicam*) from the attacks of enemies plotting the corruption of the Christian faith' (*In IV Sent.*, dist. 49, q. 5, a.3, quaest. 2, ad 11). In this ancient history is repeating itself.

Nevertheless, although it is the traditional doctrine of the Church that 'people suffer for Christ not only if they suffer for faith in Christ, but also if they suffer for any work of justice for love of Christ' (Thomas, *In Ep ad Rom.*, c. VIII, lect. 7), and although this doctrine is included in chapters XI-XXII on martyrdom in the *canonical* work of Benedict XIV, 'On the beatification of servants of God and the canonisation of *beati*' (*Dict. de théol. cath.*, X-8, 223-233); although Jesus proclaims blessed those who are persecuted for justice' sake, martyrdom today in Latin America is a stumbling-block to power and the ecclesiastical circles still connected with it. It is a stumbling-block because the martyrs come from a Church which has emigrated from its home among the powerful to the impoverished masses. Not everyone sees the logic of choices with the clarity of Archbishop Romero: 'Notice that the conflict is not between the Church and the government. It is between the government and the people. The Church is with the people and the people is with the Church. Thanks be to God!'[21]

It is natural that the powers which rule the earth should not allow the struggle of the poor for justice—what they call 'terrorism'—the same legitimacy as they allowed, for example, to the resistance of the rich European nations to the Nazis.

Among the faithful people, however, martyrdom within this struggle is recognised with the same spontaneity as that reflected in the ancient Acts of the Martyrs (see *Lexikon für Theologie und Kirche* VII, 134). Before God and history it may be that what will prevail will be, not the silent prudence of a hierarchy which, while it recognises its martyrs, does not question the legitimacy of those who murder them,[22] but the cry of the martyr Archbishop Romero, who, on the eve of his murder, dared to preach in these words: 'I should like to make an appeal . . . to the bases of the National Guard, of the

D

police, of the army. Brothers, you are from our own people. You are killing your own brother *campesinos*. . . . It is high time you recovered your consciences and obeyed your consciences rather than a sinful order. . . . In the name of God, yes, and in the name of this suffering people whose groans rise to heaven more loudly every day, I beg you, I ask you, I order you in the name of God—stop the repression!'[23]

No apostolic succession is genuine except at the foot of Christ's cross.[24] In the midst of the unjust and repressive order of this world we may recall the dangerous memory of today's Latin American martyrs, who are making irrevocable the only Christian fruitfulness to which Jesus, the Lord, referred: 'Unless a grain of wheat falls into the earth and dies, it remains alone; but if it dies, it bears abundant fruit. He who loves his life loses it, and he who hates his life in this world will keep it for eternal life' (John 12:24-25).

Translated by Francis McDonagh

Notes

1. J. Sobrino 'Persecución a la Iglesia en Centroamérica' *Estudios Centroamericanos* (*ECA*), San Salvador, 393 (1981), 657.

2. International Ecumenical Congress of Theology, Final Document: S. Torres, J. Eagleson *The Challenge of Basic Christian Communities* (New York 1981) p. 242.

3. I think the case of martyrdom on the missions is different, because of the cultural gulf between persecutors and martyrs.

4. Personal testimony. To be published shortly.

5. *Morir y despertar en Guatemala*, ed Ana Gispert-Sauch (CEP 1981) p. 69.

6. M. Sobrino, Cardenal Maró *La voz de los sin voz, La palabra viva de Monsenor Romero* (San Salvador, UCA 1980) p. 257. Cited below as: Romero.

7. J. Hernández Pico 'El ángulo tenebroso del martirio' *Dialogo* 51 (Guatemala 1980) 26-29.

8. Romero, 461.

9. *Ibid*, 453.

10. J. Mateos, J. Barreto *El Evangélio de Juan* (Madrid 1979) pp. 168-169.

11. E. Bloch *Das Prinzip Hoffnung* (Frankfurt am Main 1959). References are to the Spanish edition, *El Principio Esperanza* (Madrid 1980). Here, p. 275.

12. Bloch, p. 277.

13. Bloch, p. 497.

14. Bloch, p. 275.

15. Bloch, p. 481.

16. Bloch, p. 277.

17. Bloch, p. 279.

18. K. Marx quoted by Bloch, p. 501.

19. Romero, p. 455.

20. See Puebla, paras 92, 265, 668, 1138, and see para. 87, where the words 'martyrs' and 'martyrdom' are avoided. See also the 'Note on Martyrdom' in the Working Document prepared by CELAM in 1978.

21. Romero, p. 455.

22. Ana Gispert-Sauch in the work cited in note 5, p. 118.

23. Romero, 291; also in *Romero: Martyr for Liberation* (London 1982) pp. 31-32.

24. J. Moltmann *Kirche in der Kraft des Geistes* (Munich 1975, Spanish ed.) pp. 418-419.

Maurice Barth

Basic Communities Facing Martyrdom: Testimonies from the Churches of Central America

Book of Wisdom 1:13-14: 'God did not make death, and he does not delight in the death of the living.'
    A leaflet distributed in the streets of San Salvador in 1978: 'Work for reconstruction: kill a priest.'

SAN SALVADOR 1979, Sunday, eight in the morning, in the cathedral. People everywhere, mostly ordinary poor people. Suddenly a wave of applause sweeps through the concrete nave. A short man comes forward in priestly vestments. He is about to celebrate mass and deliver a homily lasting over an hour, punctuated by applause. It will be a homily classical in style, but nevertheless 'extra-ordinary', different from what the poor people have been hearing for centuries, trapped as they have been in a religion of submission and hope—hope for the next life. It will be different because it will be both the good news proclaimed *to* the poor and *their* word, arising out of the daily dialogues with a bishop who shares their day-to-day anxieties. It will be a homily which is a constant appeal to transcendence, considered not as an abstract notion or disembodied spirituality, but as an entry into a new world, a transfiguration of man, as individual and as a people, now. He used to invite his people to take part in that transfiguration, that liberation: 'Transcendent hope must be maintained by the signs of historical hope, even if they are signs as simple in appearance as those proclaimed by the prophet Isaiah when he says, "They shall build their houses and live in them. They shall plant vines and eat their fruits." ' But 'this defence of the poor in a world in serious conflict has introduced a new fact into the recent history of our Church, persecution'.[1] This persecution claimed Archbishop Romero as its most famous victim, but his murder was unfortunately no more than an episode in the struggle waged systematically against the Latin American Church. 'If they have done this with the most prominent representatives of the Church,' the archbishop continued, referring to the nine priests murdered at this time, 'you will easily understand what has happened to ordinary Christians, the peasants, catechists and delegates of the word,[2] the basic ecclesial communities. Among them the number of people threatened, kidnapped, tortured and murdered is in the thousands. But the most important thing is to look at why the Church has been persecuted. Not just any priest has

43

been persecuted, not just any institution has been attacked. Attack and persecution have been concentrated on the part of the Church which has taken the side of the poor in our country and defended them. . . . Persecution is nothing other than sharing the fate of the poor. . . . When the Church organised and united to reflect on the hopes and sufferings of the poor, it suffered the same fate as Jesus, persecution.' In fact, between 1970 and 1981 in El Salvador, eleven priests, one bishop and five nuns were murdered. In July 1982, as a result of the persecution, 50 per cent of parishes had no administrator.

The report of the Pax Christi mission estimates that 'the present persecution has reached such a pitch of ferocity as to effectively reduce the Church to silence'.[3] The development of the guerilla movement, which has effective control of over a third of the country, and the increase in the number of refugees, both outside and inside the country (more than 800,000 in July 1982) have radically transformed the structures of the country. The basic communities are re-establishing themselves in the areas controlled by the opposition and in the refugee camps, but the camps are not immune to military incursions, even in the surrounding countries.

Extracts from a message from the basic Christian communities of San Salvador to 'the Christians of the other parts of the world' (May 1982): 'You know that our Church has suffered much in order to be faithful to the mission of Jesus. . . . In this situation entire communities have left their areas. Their houses and the churches have been destroyed. Our catechists are constantly threatened. It has become increasingly difficult to continue our work. . . . Despite the surveillance of those who do not want us to live as "true brothers" in El Salvador,[4] we meet to celebrate our faith. We organise meetings of catechists, couples, candidates for the priesthood. We attend to the needs of our displaced brothers and sisters. . . . The eucharistic celebration is the key meeting in our communities. There we renew our Christian commitment to our people. There we meet together with our dead, our martyrs. . . . At each Sunday mass we recall the memory of sometimes as many as twenty-five brothers and sisters who have given their lives. . . . They are united with Jesus, with Archbishop Romero, and with him they are in our midst. . . .'[5]

In Guatemala many religious, catechists and delegates of the word have been murdered, for nothing more than putting their faith into practice, some even simply because of the possibility that their faith might have led them into such a commitment.[6] A document published by the Justice and Peace Committee of Guatemala puts it like this: 'Guatemala is going through the most transcendental moment of its history. The people, the poor and exploited majority . . . have realised that it is now their time and they are determined to be the shapers of their country's history. . . . Through their faith many Christians have come to see that they must struggle together with this people to overthrow the policies of death followed by the ruling clique and inaugurate policies of life, under which children can smile, run and play, under which families can live in love and, above all, under which we can say aloud that we are Christians. We want a society in which we can read the Bible, hold meetings, in which hosts are no longer buried and in which the church bells ring out to proclaim the good news that Jesus is risen among a people which has finally obtained its liberation and can celebrate, as a family, the word of God.'

Of course, to justify its plan of destruction the regime accuses the Church of being involved with 'international Communism'. In the middle of 1981 persecution had already claimed the lives of twelve priests. Ninety-one priests and sixty-four nuns had also either been expelled or forced to leave by threats, sixty parishes were without priests, the six Catholic radio stations had been destroyed, or reduced to silence, three convents and presbyteries had suffered bomb attacks, ten Catholic colleges had been destroyed or closed, thirty training centres and twelve novitiates had been closed. Countless catechists and lay people have been kidnapped or murdered.[7] The murders and physical tortures have been followed by psychological ones, as in the case of Fr. Pellecer. A government-orchestrated campaign of denigration against the Jesuits and other religious orders has had repercussions as far away as Europe.

The Pax Christi report mentioned earlier sums up the situation as follows: 'Guatemala has fifteen dioceses, of which twelve have adopted the pastoral approach of Vatican II. As a result of the repression one diocese, Quiché,[8] has almost disappeared. Its bishop has been expelled from the country. Other bishops are in practice prevented from exercising their ministry. . . . It is no exaggeration to say that the Guatemalan church is living in the catacombs.' Nevertheless, as in El Salvador, the religious orders which have suffered the worst persecution are seeing the number of vocations grow. Here are extracts from the testimony of some catechists:[9] 'One of the methods of repression is to send soldiers to ask catechists if they are Catholics. If they say yes, the soldiers start to beat them up. . . . Where they have found bibles, they have torn them up, trampled them underfoot or burned them. They say, "If you keep that up, next time we'll kill you. You have to give up the Bible." So people bury the bibles and the hymn-books, but they continue to meet, not in houses but in the mountains, in secret. Our lives are of little importance. What matters is to do something for people, to make sure our faith doesn't die. . . . The people know that the blood of the catechists bears fruit. . . . The blood of our friends is a light. . . . You ask why they are doing that to Christians? It is because we have understood what the Bible is. . . . We have begun to read the Bible and the words we read are quite clear to us. We have the story of Moses, who brought his people out of slavery, the story of Jesus, who was persecuted from childhood. . . . That is why persecution is severest against Christians, because they have realised that for us the Bible is an awakening. . . .'

Neighbouring Honduras has not been spared either, even if systematic persecution there is more recent. Since the 1978 *coup d'état* the regime has directly attacked the Church for taking the side of the poor. There have been expulsions, churches have been occupied by the army, pastoral work closely watched. The Honduran army has engaged in joint operations with the Salvadorean army to terrorise the refugee camps.

But repression is not just a tragic episode. It is the expression of an ideological battle engaged at an international level. At issue are not only the structures of a society in which the majority of the poor are no longer resigned to death from hunger (physical, cultural, political, spiritual hunger), but also a vision of the world. The economic aspect was recognised brutally by the 1969 Rockerfeller report: 'We must watch this Latin American Church carefully. If it carries out what was agreed at Medellín,[10] it will damage our interests.'

The ideological aspect of this struggle has been the object of many condemnations. 'The acts which we are denouncing are not isolated. They are the result of a process with clearly defined characteristics which is threatening to become established throughout our Latin American continent. Under the pretext of a constant and unchallengeable appeal to national security we are witnessing the steady consolidation of a model of security which stifles basic freedoms, violates the most elementary rights and subjects citizens to the dictates of a formidable and ubiquitous police state.'[11] However, 'national security' is not just a pretext; it is also a doctrine which has been taught for nearly forty years in the staff colleges of Latin America and originated in the United States. It is a vision of the nation and of the State: the individual and the people are no more than myths. The only reality is the nation, which merges with the State, which represents power. The world is simply the scene of a struggle (economic, ideological, cultural, military), in which everyone must take part. Everyone is friend or foe. (Today it is the battle between Communist society and western society.) Christianity is no more than a set of symbols giving rise to gestures (a practice) and a morality which contribute to the national sense of identity. During 1974 a document addressed to military and political leaders was circulating in Latin America which contained specific instructions for action against the Church; these are now being implemented daily. In May 1980 a group of experts working for the US Republican Party produced a document (the 'Santa Fe document') proposing 'A new inter-American policy for the Eighties' which includes the following statement: 'US foreign policy must begin to challenge (and not simply react to) the theology of liberation.' In April 1981, again in the United States, the 'Institute on Religion and Democracy' was set up with the US ambassador to the United Nations, Mrs Jean Kirkpatrick, as one of the leading members. Its specific task—amply funded—is to devise a strategy in the religious sphere, which is seen as a crucial area for political-ideological struggle. In May 1981 the Institute announced the launching of a campaign against the role of the Church in Central America and affirmed its support for the Salvadorean junta.

The sufferings of Latin American Christians are intensified by the incomprehension of some members of the hierarchy, and by the very complicity of some with the dictators and torturers. Bishops have justified torture, called for the expulsion of foreign religious and accepted ranks in the army. The Pax Christi report was attacked by the Latin American Episcopal Conference. There is an attempt to create a silence round the memory of Archbishop Romero, or to belittle him, while the ordinary people invoke him as a saint.

The people, however, have entered a new and historic stage in their journey of faith. Undaunted by the persecutions and the compromises of some of the hierarchy, they know where their Church and their hope are to be found.

> And my Church has come out of the sacristy.
> It has stopped spending its time sprinkling holy water
>   like poor people's medicine. . . .
> It has realised that it has to choose between
>   the sacristy and the world. . . .
> And because of that it has gone down into hell. . . .
> They have killed many of my Church's children,
>   but not the message they proclaimed. . . .
> And my Church continues on its way.
> And people will be free. . . .
> My Church is salvation for many. . . .
> That is my Church.

[Extracts from a litany used by the basic communities of El Salvador, translated from the French of DIAL, No 674.]

Translated by Francis McDonagh

Notes

1. Speech delivered by Archbishop Romero at the University of Louvain on 2 February 1980 when he received an honorary doctorate.
2. Lay men and women who preside at celebrations when there are no priests.
3. Report of the Pax Christi International Mission to Guatemala, 4 vols, *Honduras, Nicaragua, El Salvador, Guatemala,* (Antwerp, Belgium 1982).
4. The diocese of San Salvador is in the area controlled by the Government.
5. Before the war El Salvador had a population of around 5,000,000. There was one priest for every 10,000 inhabitants.

6. Mgr. L. Bettazzi, in the common introduction to the Pax Christi reports.

7. Justice and Peace Committee, August 1981.

8. The diocese of Quiché is composed basically of Indians. Guatemala has about 7,000,000 people.

9. Translated from the French text in DIAL (*Diffusion Amérique Latine*) No 107. This testimony is from women catechists.

10. The epoch-making assembly of the Latin American Episcopal Conference in 1968 which committed the Church to work for social justice.

11. Declaration of the Chilean Episcopal Conference, 17 August 1976. Translated from the French of DIAL, No 340.

Pedro Casaldáliga

The 'Crucified' Indians—A Case of Anonymous Collective Martyrdom

BY MARTYRDOM, do we mean a confession-witness-to-the-death to Christian faith or to faith in the kingdom? This is one question that has to be decided at the outset.

In answering it, the following four considerations should be borne in mind:

(1) The witness of martyrdom is a witness brought about by violence, even when it is given willingly for the faith professed.

(2) This witness is valid to the extent that it is given as such and recognised as such. We must be receptive to the martyrdoms going on around us today. The Church tends sometimes to lose its receptivity to certain martyrdoms.

(3) People today are more ready to canonise not so much martyrs to a faith, which may be a private matter to them, as those public victims of any sort of imperialism and repression.

(4) The Catholic Church has taken into its martyrology, which has not always been historically critical, the martyrdom of collectivities, more or less anonymous. There are collective martyrdoms; there are martyr peoples.

1. MARTYRDOM ON A CONTINENTAL SCALE

In my introduction to *Mass for a World Without Evils*[1] I wrote: 'We Christians are used to recognising and celebrating only the martyrs that others have made of us. We quietly ignore the many martyrs we have made.

'Here in Brazil, 1978 was "The Year of Martyrs" for the Indian cause. We were celebrating the 350th anniversary of the three Jesuit martyrs of Rio Grande: Roque Gonzalez, Alfonso Rodriguez and João Castilhos. The Indigenous Missionary Council decided that justice demanded that the death of the three Jesuit missionaries should hardly be celebrated. Because the dead were far more numerous. We should also be celebrating the deaths of thousands of Indians, sacrificed to the Christian empires of Spain and Portugal. Both (missionary priests and the Indians themselves) martyrs of the Indigenous Cause (martyrs, I should say, for the kingdom). The cross (loved, used or imposed) stood in the midst of them all. The former, dying for the love of Christ. The latter, massacred "in the name" of Christ and the Emperor. . . .'

The massacre of the indigenous peoples—of entire peoples—over the whole of the

48

American continent, coincided, year after year, with the arrival, presence and actions of the European colonisers and the successive empires that came to dominate the land of America. From the first galleons, through the exportation of mineral wealth, to absentee landlords, hydro-electric schemes and multinational mining corporations, the relationship of the white westerners, 'Christians' and 'civilisers', to the Indians, 'savages', 'discovered' and 'conquered', has always been one of violence, depredation and extermination.

The invaders arbitrarily divided up the land of America, with no consideration for the sacred rights of the real sons and lords of that land. And they reduced the many and varied aboriginal peoples, each with their own culture and history, to the collective anonymity of 'Indians'. . . . 'Our sufferings began with the first ship that came to Brazil', declared Sempre, a Xerente Indian.[2] 'Brazil was not discovered, Brazil was stolen', as Marçal, a Guaraní Indian, explained to Pope John Paul II at that memorable meeting in Manaus in July 1980.

America, as an indigenous continent, has over the centuries been systematically expropriated and crucified by bearers of the cross. The massacre has been continuous and on a continental scale.

Today this massacre of the indigenous peoples is still going on, in more or less 'civilised' forms, even in Latin American countries whose population still has an indigenous majority. As an example one can take the very present tragedy—which the western Christian world manages to watch without remorse, or with a greater degree of connivance—going on in Guatemala. This is what the Indigenous Missionary Council reported on 5 July last year, after hearing the report of its secretary-general, Fr. Paulo Suess, who had been there on a visit: 'The indigenous peoples of Guatemala, who represent 60 per cent of the population of the country, are being made the victims of systematic massacres. There are daily assassinations and destructions, not only of individuals, but of entire villages. They are using the "cleared land" principle tried out in Vietnam.'

The document goes on to state that the massacres 'are carried out either by the army, advised by Israeli "technicians", or by para-military groups. They are even arming Indians against other Indians in the army itself and in the vigilante patrols. . . . Virtually all the military equipment comes from Israel, the tactical sub-agent of North American geo-politics.' The situation today in Guatemala, the report continues is 'the most serious current eruption of a chronic global crisis which exists in both Americas, where the indigenous peoples have become the object of outside interests, with their consequent expulsion or assassination. This is now set for the final solution, the genocide of the indegenous peoples on a continental scale.'

Specific accusations are levelled at leading figures in Guatemala, including the present President Ephraim Ríos Montt (who calls himself 'God's emissary'), who 'in 1973 led the massacre of the Indians of Sansrisay' and his Minister Ricardo Méndez Ruíz, who 'directed the most violent campaign against the Indians (especially the Quicho and Pocoma) that the country has seen'.

Putting together the common causes and pointing out the common collective disaster they represent, the International Conference of Non-Governmental Bodies of the United Nations on Discrimination Against the Indigenous Peoples of Latin America in 1977, declared: 'The representatives of the indigenous peoples made clear to the international community how discrimination, genocide and ethnocide were being carried out. Though the situation varies from country to country, its roots are common to all: they include brutal colonisation to open a way for the sacking of their lands and their natural resources, since commercial interests operate for the sake of maximum profit; the massacre of millions of natives over the centuries and the continued appropriation of their lands, depriving them of the possibility of developing their own resources and livelihoods; the denial of self-determination to indigenous peoples and nations, with the destruction of their systems of values and social and cultural structures. The situation clearly shows that this oppression is continuing, and its results are expressed in the destruction of the indigenous nations.'[3]

2. THE PROCESS IN BRAZIL

I should like to quote some data concerning the Indian tragedy in Brazil, which is closer to home for me. First, it is worth noting that Brazilian literature calls the Indian *Y-Juca-Pirama*—'he who must die'.

It has been calculated that there were about 5,000,000 natives in this land of *Pau-brasil* when Pedro Alvares Cabral 'discovered' it to the greed of the 'civilising' West. Today, in Catholic, civilised Brazil, there are about 220,000 Indians left. These are 'they who have come out of the great tribulation' (Rev. 7:14), the 'remnant' who have just managed to escape the greed of the 'idol of the invader' (Dan. 9:27).

According to the anthropologist Melatti, eighty-seven tribal groups disappeared in Brazil between the years 1900 and 1957.

The Karaja Indians, who live almost exclusively within my diocese of São Félix do Araguaia, were 10,000 strong at the beginning of this century; now they are down to under 1,500.

'White hand against the Cinza People' is the title of a recent pamphlet[4] published as a cry to alert public opinion to the dramatic situation of the Nambiquara Indians, threatened by a highway financed by the World Bank and surrounded by estates run from outside for profit. The back cover of the pamphlet asks us to put ourselves in the situation of these Indians faced with extermination: 'One day, the city in which you have lived since time immemorial is invaded by "civilised" beings. By force of arms which you have never seen or dreamt of, your people are thrown out. Those who resist are killed. Those who do not resist will die later as a result of illnesses they never knew before, from hunger or just from sadness. . . . They call your music barbarous and barbarous the—happy—life your people have lived for thousands of years! You used to work for yourself; now you will have to work for "them"—and they will clear the area of vagabonds.

Suddenly they introduce you to "revolutionary" concepts—moral, economic, to do with your everyday life. They flourish their beliefs, despise everything that made you a Man worthy of this "garden of *Tupã*" (the Indian word for God). They call this pretty names like Progress, National Interest, Civilising Process. They name streets and squares after the people they have exterminated, in homage.

There were 20,000 (Nambiquara Indians) at the beginning of this century. Now they are down to 650.'

The representatives of various indigenous peoples of Brazil, meeting in the ruins of São Miguel Rio Grande do Sul, on the 'Day of the Indian', 19 April 1977, declared: 'First we want to say that 22 April 1500, the day Pedro Alvares Cabral first set foot on these shores, was the first day of the expansion of western civilisation and the beginning of the end of the indigenous societies.

'As the years went by, the process of our destruction was intensified, carried out by western civilisation. This used every means to degrade and massacre the groups of Indians. The process was helped by diseases introduced by the white man, previously unknown amongst us, by expropriation from our lands, by the application of systems of colonialist-ethnocentric education which did not respect our political, economic and religious structure. . . .'

3. THE INDIANS AND THE CHURCH

These examples suffice to show the scale of the human—biological, cultural and spiritual—tragedy to which the whole Amerindian continent was reduced by the civilising system of the West, made up of domination and exploitation, ethnocentrism and racism, economic colonialism and religious proselytism.

For some time—since, in fact, I first came into everyday contact with the native populations—I have felt the disappearance of whole peoples as an absurd mystery of historical iniquity, which reduces me to the most abject sort of faith: 'Lord, why have you abandoned us?' How can the Bread of Life, the creative Spirit of every culture, allow these multiple annihilations. . .?

For us Christians, for the churches as churches, this Indian tragedy is a historical accusation which has never been made strongly enough. It ought to bring us remorse, to be a prophetic and effective convulsion for us. Because we were far more persecutors than persecuted. . . .

The willingness of many missionaries to face death, the charitable and 'educational' works of the missions, the isolated protests of a few like de Las Casas in the past or the tardy protest that some churches—still isolated—are making today against this continental-scale massacre, cannot redeem the Church—the churches—from a historical sin of omission and connivance, which can only be compared to that other historical sin—perhaps even greater—committed by the same churches in the face of the Negro slave trade. . . .

I was amazed when Rome sent letters of disapproval of the 'mass for a world without evils' (a celebration for the Indians) and the 'Quilombo mass' (a Black celebration), on the grounds that a Eucharist could never be used to claim the rights of one people. . . . (How many Eucharists have we—priests, bishops and popes—not celebrated to commemorate some doubtful civic or military event or to give thanks for some—probably sacrilegious—gift from a prince or an empress or a *madame*!) As if the Eucharist were not always the paschal celebration of a Liberation and a 'dangerous memory' of the Death of one killed by the 'powers of this world'!

The Church will only be an announcement of the kingdom to the extent that it is a denouncement of the anti-kingdom. And it can only be a witness to Pardon and Grace insofar as it is penitent and forgiving. 'The announcement of the Good News can never be made in the context of the Bad News of a robbery and invasion of native lands, the extinction of their cultures, paternalistic and oppressive practices. The Good News cannot be proclaimed without denouncing genocide and ethnocide. But proclamation and denunciation must be preceded by renunciation, by the conversion of the whole missionary Church. . . .'[5]

'Evangelising' has become too much like 'civilising', 'westernising', 'integrating'.

Some great missionaries to the Americas, to Asia and to Africa, shunned by the official Church because of the suspicion aroused by their actions, did know how to show a greater sensitivity in preaching the Gospel. They refuse to transmit a culture in the process of evangelisation. They came in the guise of a servant, as Jesus is presented in the Letter to the Philippians. They would not lend themselves to the martyrdom of the peoples to whom they were sent.

The Gospel can never be the substitution of one culture by another, but must be the force that transforms any culture from within, the soul of a people, a collective dynamic fact, capable of free eschatological sublimation. Missiology should take another look at the analyses made, very ethnocentrically, in its past, of the reactions of peoples it called 'pagan'. Then it might find the real reasons why these martyred peoples reacted against those strangers who invaded their lands and their soul, their language and their myths. In the name of a 'true' God, a supposedly false God was killed and is being killed, and the spirits and also the bodies of those who adore him are killed, with whole cultures and peoples being wiped out. We are responsible for the martyrdom of others as much as we should glory in our own!

In 1628 the Guaraní chief Potivara told his people to stand up to the 'missionary' Jesuit Roque Gonzalez, because he felt him to represent a great threat to 'our ancient being' and to the 'customs of our country'; because the missionary wanted to introduce 'gods we have not heard of', the 'god of the Spaniards', the 'empty Christian rituals', in place of 'our true deities'; a 'foreign lie' in place of 'our paternal truth'. . . . And in our days a Kayabi Indian, Mairauê, has lamented, in sorrowing religious tones, at a gathering of Indian chiefs: 'Once the Whites came, the whole of our life began to be threatened. Our holy places were profaned. We used to be able to have our festivals and paint ourselves, run races, sing and play the *hukahuka*. With the white man all this has gone.'[6]

4. CONCLUSION

The Church in the Americas and the Church in Europe need to do an about-turn, with a new spirit of incarnation and listening, in the face of this martyrdom-massacre and this cry-message from these crucified peoples. From this Galilee of the Gentiles a liberating light is shining!

Amerindia still has 40,000,000 survivors, with their own identity, deeply religious, regular worshippers of the God of Nature and of Life, rich in community and bearers of the seeds of the Word. 'Remnant' of a great martyr people, which no one can now count because it no longer exists in its greatness, but which paradoxically possesses the evangelising power of an age-old collective martyrdom.

This martyrdom, the fruit of our hands, and this identity, a fruitful alternative for our hollow society, call us to conversion. 'Their abandoned and marginalised condition, deprived of all power, makes us see clearly that these minorities must be, through the power of the Spirit, a source of renewal for the whole people of God and for human society in general.'[7]

Translated by Paul Burns

Notes

1. *Missa de terra sem males*, published by CEDI (Rio de Janeiro 1980).
2. 'Semana do Indio, 82' (CNBB/CIMI—the Indigenous Missionary Council) p. 19.
3. Final Resolution of the Conference, 23 Sep. 1977, quoted by P. Suess, *Em defesa dos Povos Indigenas: Documentos e Legislação* (São Paulo 1980) p. 78.
4. 'Mão branca contra o Povo Cinza' (São Paulo 1980).
5. Suess, in the work cited in note 3, at p. 12.
6. 'Semana . . .' cited in note 2.
7. Suess, in the work cited in note 3, at p. 68.

Vàclav Mali

On the Situation of the Church in the CSSR

WHAT FOLLOWS is an attempt to outline the life and position of the Catholic Church in present-day, 'normalised' Czechoslovakia. It is an attempt to give the western reader, whose ideas about the life of believers in actual socialist countries are often based on superficial and patchy information, a better grasp of how things really are. This is not a comprehensive report; no exhaustive statistics are adduced, except a few of the most important figures; these are useful illustrations but do not guarantee that the situation has been correctly understood.

If we want to understand the Church's present situation we must first look into the past. Within the structure of the Austrian monarchy, to which Bohemia and Slovakia earlier belonged, the Catholic Church had a privileged position prior to the First World War, not only because of the number of its adherents but through its social influence. It was a State Church, supported and advantaged financially as well as politically by Imperial power. State power and Church power were interdependent, entwined, forming an indivisible whole. Following the establishment of the autonomous Czechoslovak Republic in 1918 the long-standing antipathy to the Catholic Church suddenly manifested itself. About a million of the faithful and 300 priests left the Church. The watchword 'Freedom from Rome' was symbolic of Czech inebriation with freedom; the Slovaks were less concerned to break the identity of State and Church power. But because of the attitude of the hierarchy there was no separation of Church and State. The Church continued to be supported financially by the State, though it was no longer involved in State affairs. The Church leaders' fear of independence and their unwillingness to give up their dependence on the State was to be fateful in the end.

After the *coup d'état* of 1948 the Communists made use of this situation in their anti-Church politics. The legal relations between the Church and the new political power were expressed in Law 218/49 concerning the economic security of churches and religious communities. This law formed the basis for the Government Measures 219-223/49. Church property was confiscated. The law establishes the State's right to superintend the Church's finances, which are provided by the State. By various internal measures this superintendence was then extended to all the Church's activity, including spiritual matters. Practically every one of the Church's public functions requires the State's prior permission. Priests are given this permission only for a particular place: it can be withdrawn at any time without reason. For instance special permission is needed

53

for various Church celebrations and pilgrimages, retreats and ordinations, religious instruction, religious publications, contact with other countries, the appointment of teachers and admission of students to the theological faculty, etc. The position of the hierarchy is unenviable. It cannot decide freely according to Church laws, but has continually to fight strenuously for most elementary necessities of Church life— services, the appointment of priests, etc. Every Church activity is controlled by the State according to its own needs and aims. In the Fifties hundreds of Catholic priests were imprisoned contrary to the law, on a variety of pretexts and for many years; all resident bishops were interned for the whole period; the activities of all orders were prohibited and almost all order priests were arrested; ecclesiastical publishing houses were closed down and many active laypeople in different Catholic associations were given long sentences; all diocesan seminaries were abolished and replaced by two national seminaries under State control. Gradually people came back from prison, but this brutal attack had left permanent wounds; the Church's continuity was broken.

As well as having continually to come to grips with this baleful legacy one is faced with constant pressure and endless stratagems on the part of the State. What practical opportunities do we have for influencing our society? The aim of the ruling ideology is clear: 'to win every citizen of our society for the scientific world view', in the words of spokesmen for the State. Believers are merely tolerated. All the mass media carry on a deliberate propaganda, distorting the nature of Christianity and preferring to avoid all mention of religion whatsoever. This is taken so far that in our country, as far as possible, no Church buildings must appear on picture postcards (with a few exceptions in Prague). The State is vigilant to ensure that the Church's activity is limited to the area of cult: services, the administration of the sacraments, funerals. Anything beyond this is punishable. Each local town has a Secretary for Church Affairs, an official with practically unlimited power of interfering in the work of priests, who for their part are responsible to him. He can revoke their State licence without giving any reason—even where, for instance, the priest is simply being too energetic and his congregations are increasing. The authorities tolerate a certain amount of initiative with regard to repairing Church buildings, indeed they welcome it to some extent (for the sake of tourism, etc.); it means that the parish priest is kept busy; but here, too—if for instance his industriousness begins to have an effect on the vicinity—he can get into difficulties. Today there are about 3,000 priests officiating and about 200-250 without a State licence, working in other occupations.

Religious instruction is allowed only in schools and depends, for instance, on whether enough children explicitly register for it with their parents' written confirmation. The ruling ideology's claim to be the sole influence on youth allows no compromise. As soon as it is discovered that the children are being influenced by Christianity, the other teachers have to increase the usual anti-religious propaganda and thus bring their personal authority into play. Parents who send their children to religious instruction risk difficulties in their work: they cannot have any position of responsibility, undertake business trips abroad, etc., and they must accept the fact that their child will not be admitted to third level education, for it will always be in his personal file that he has attended religious instruction. Parents have no religious books, for the only religious publishers, Charita for Bohemia and Spolok Sv. Vojtěcha for Slovakia, are only permitted one publication per year. Believers can scarcely get hold of a bible, since (for Catholics) it has not been reprinted for years and is simply not available. The Church periodicals—one weekly for laity and one monthly for priests—publish no news of theological issues in the world, Bible studies, help for children's instruction, but mostly keep to peripheral issues acceptable to the State (e.g., the 'peace' ideology).

The number of students at both theological faculties is continually being reduced—e.g., this year, of sixty-five applicants in Litoměrice only thirty-five were accepted. Before being accepted applicants often have to undergo interrogation by the security authorities, who evaluate them according to their own criteria. Often the professors are insufficiently qualified and are only appointed because of their loyalty to the State. The level and methods of training are inadequate to the needs of modern theological work and pastoral care.

Only five out of the twelve dioceses in the CSSR are supervised by bishops (Prague, Olomouc, Trnava, Nitra, Banska Bystrica), the others by vicars capitular. Although the Orders were never abolished, their work is prohibited and men are not allowed to live together. Where they have permission they act as diocesan priests and may not wear the habit of their Order. The lay brothers work in civilian occupations and have not had any vocations for more than thirty years. Retired sisters mostly live together in supervised homes for old people; those who can work do so mostly in institutions for mentally ill children and in old people's homes, but they are often driven out of these positions, lest they should have a positive effect on their environment. Vocation work is likewise forbidden.

A special role in the life of the Church is played by the priests' association Pacem in terris, which continues the work of the earlier Priests' Peace Movement (1950-1968). Under the pretext of being a peace movement this association is an effective instrument of the State against the Church. These priests are silent on all the real Church–State problems and help to create the impression that there are none. What the power of the State does not want to say or do itself, it achieves through this movement. Following the declaration of the Congregation for the Clergy of March 1982, which applies among others to this movement, a virulent campaign against the Vatican arose in the official propaganda, designed to keep this association alive. About one-third of active priests belong to it; Cardinal Tomášek was never a member, and Bishop Vrana (Olomouc), Vicar Kavale (České Budějovice) and Vicar Horký (Brno) have recently left it; the situation in Slovakia is less clear: some priests are leaving the movement, many stay to wait and see what will happen.

Can this list of limitations sum up the real life of the Church in Czechoslovakia? By no means. People's natural need and yearning for the deeper life which faith gives cannot be suppressed and is always finding ways of expression. Many of the faithful do not restrict themselves to Church services but form vigorous groups and circles led by a priest or layperson, coming together for Bible studies, addresses, and to deepen their religious formation; they go on outings or on holiday together, which takes the place of the proscribed retreats. Often these encounters take place right across the churches and thus become the only really fruitful kind of ecumenism. Mutual recognition and prayer in common strengthen the awareness that brothers and sisters of different churches need each other. For the most part the spiritual orientation is towards a good Christian life which shows itself in a wide range of caring activities (looking after the old, supporting the larger families, etc.). The lack of religious literature is partly countered by religious *samizdat* consisting of translations and original material, circulated only with great sacrifice. There are also periodical newsletters; the whole scene is so rich and varied that one can hardly appreciate it all.

Recent years have also seen the spread of the Charismatic Movement, which inspires a spontaneity which is otherwise so painfully absent in all aspects of our life. The example of the Brotherhood of Taizé also has an influence, especially on young people. Priests, who are only allowed to meet officially at vicariate conferences, under the supervision of the Secretary, are feeling more and more that their demanding work urgently requires a real sense of unity which is not achieved by official statements. The silenced religious communities, too, refuse to be consigned totally to passivity, and are accepting new members and trying afresh to implement the original aims of their Order under difficult conditions. The Focolare Movement is also spreading among priests. All this contributes to the variety of the Church's expressions.

Secretly ordained priests are also at work among the faithful—mostly in Slovakia. But there is no 'underground Church' as such. All unofficial spiritual activities are simply to supply the lack of other possibilities and take place in the awareness of the need for a visible unity of Christians, of one Church.

The Catholic Church is still numerically the strongest Church in the CSSR. Today about 40-50 per cent of the population of Bohemia are baptised Catholics, in Moravia they are 70 per cent and in Slovakia about 90 per cent. Structurally the Church is bound to the Vatican, a place outside the 'iron curtain'. The proximity of Poland with its 95 per cent of Catholics arouses exaggerated fears in the corridors of State power. The fact that the variety of independently functioning, unofficial spiritual activities cannot be monitored and are not under central control only serves to aggravate the fears of the authorities about the influence and power of the Catholic Church, which latterly has again become public enemy number one. Of course, as a result of its own power-complex the State authority greatly over-estimates the Catholic Church's potential strength. But it remains true that, as the only public and organised communities within the socialist society, our churches do represent and—albeit feebly—proclaim a different ideology, that they have a different view of man's vocation and different answers to the questions his life poses than those who adhere to the official ideology (which has recently become more threadbare and bloodless). This is why the authorities have become more nervous about everything which might have an appeal for people, which might call into question the 'normalised' view of the world and of things. Thus greater pressure is brought to bear on priests and laity, there is an increase in interrogations, house-searchings and arrests. Last year even the homes for retired priests and religious in Kadaň and Moravec were searched.

Has this then given an exhaustive account of the Church's real situation? With all due respect and reverence for what is alive in the Church, we must also look at the interior of the Church's body and not see it only in its confrontation with the State. The western reader is given the impression that the whole problem of the Church's difficult situation in the socialist State lies exclusively in the authorities' ever-tightening and ever more subtle grip, silencing the Church; as if the Church is only hindered from proclaiming its message effectively and credibly by the collaborating activities of Pacem in terris and by the unlimited compromising of bishops. This is only partly true.

The Church is also to blame for the crises and difficulties it experiences and suffers. Its silence on important social problems—such as military service, human rights, etc.; its manipulation of the consciences of believers by authoritarian decisions; conservatism in its customs and clinging to tradition—understood as a sterile repetition of the past; the over-hasty suspecting of heresy where people are only trying to proclaim the Gospel in a modern form; inappropriate self-pity and acting on sufferance; constantly bringing up old scores, which shows that people have not come to terms with them; the over-emphasis on an exemplary moral life—as if it were the sum of the Christian message; the longing to survive, *vis-à-vis* the intellectual and social chaos which surrounds us, by keeping behind walls of accepted norms, afraid to let go; the reserve and reticence, constraint and hypocrisy, which make impossible any genuine discussion in matters of faith; distrust of the freer theology of the West and an over-evaluation of one's own experience; the eager affirmation of the Church as an authoritative institution which possesses the truth, to which the others who have gone astray have only to return: these are all characteristic ways of thought, speech and action of many believers and priests who otherwise, in an unofficial capacity, take many courageous risks. It is all too reminiscent of the manner and pattern of official propaganda—this is precisely the real kernel of the Church's problematic position. This inner crisis is only exacerbated by external pressure.

Until this Church experiences a complete inner renewal in the Spirit of the Gospel, it cannot contribute much to a healing of society, despite all its intense and well-meant activity. An inner lack of credibility will have no appeal, even if external pressure is relaxed. A period of external oppression offers the opportunity for a genuine revaluation of former attitudes, for purification and a readiness for unreserved sacrifice. Then the Church could fulfil her mission and hand on the message of Jesus in its integrity. That is where its hope lies, not in a mere survival for better times without oppression and external limitations.

Translated by Graham Harrison

E

Walbert Bühlmann

The Church as Institution in the Context of Persecution

TODAY WE know that there were not as many martyrs in the first three centuries as was long believed on the basis of the apologetic writings of the time; we also know that there are more martyrs today than people generally suspect. How does the Church as an institution react where Christians are persecuted?[1]

1. BASIC CONSIDERATIONS

(a) The individual martyr fears martyrdom and naturally holds back because of the drive for self-preservation, man's strongest instinct; yet at the same time, in virtue of higher motivation and grace he courageously and calmly accepts it. So the Church, as institution, lives in a dialectical tension in the face of martyrdom: on the one hand, throughout history, it has rejoiced in the martyrs' triumph[2] (though today we know that this is no definitive proof of truth, for Communism, too, has its warriors and martyrs and celebrates them); on the other hand it must revolt against and denounce the persecution and killing of Christians, seeking to stop it with all the institutional means at its disposal.

(b) We must humbly admit that as an institution the Church itself has persecuted Christians for centuries, i.e., the so-called heretics, who claimed to be good Christians and took the Gospel as their basis. The Church not only condemned heresy but heretics too, and if the Inquisition convicted them of error they were handed over to the power of the State and hence also to torture and often to death.[3]

(c) Since the Second Vatican Council one can see wave upon wave of a growing readiness in the Church to commit itself to the poor, the exploited, the marginalised and the persecuted. It was heralded by the two encyclicals of Pius XI *Divini Redemptoris* and *Mit brennender Sorge*. Then came the famous speech of Cardinal Lercaro on behalf of the poor in the first Council Session which triggered off the 'Church of the poor' movement, and *Gaudium et Spes*. A new impetus was given by the 1968 Latin-American Church Assembly of Medellín, which intended to apply the Council to that continent and clearly opted for the poor. In preparation for the 1971 Synod of Bishops on Justice in the World and in the Church, all the bishops' conferences of the world discussed this topic in detail. Above all the two popes Paul VI and John Paul II expressed themselves in documents and addresses more and more in favour of human rights and in particular of religious freedom. It was rightly said of them that they stood on the right in Church issues, but in socio-political questions they were more on the left. The World Council of Churches was not behindhand in this development. It was responsible for declarations and actions which were in part even more courageous. The public conscience has been so sensitised towards human rights that even the UN, on 10 December 1981, could pass a declaration against religious intolerance.

(d) In the institutional Church's attitude to infringements of human rights one can distinguish the prophetic from the diplomatic charisma. The prophet cries aloud, accuses, condemns, but because of his harsh speech people mostly do not listen to him. Often he is killed, but after his death his concern is vindicated. The prophet testifies that intramundane solutions are not the only ones. The diplomat puts forward the same issue in a more amicable and cautious manner. He tries to maintain bridges, not to condemn systems as such but to stay in contact with people in systems both right and left, hoping thus to improve these systems from within.

Both approaches are justifiable. They complement and need each other. It is the Church's strength that it can speak and proceed in different ways. Basically one could say that the Vatican and the apostolic nunciatures have to exercise more the diplomatic function whereas the local bishops, priests, religious and laity have to take on more the prophetic role. But there can be no absolute distinction here. Even a nuncio can act prophetically, but he does so under the seal of confidentiality without exposing the other party; and in the interests of the issue itself the prophet ought not to be totally unversed in the art of diplomacy. A good example of this complementarity was to be seen in Franco's Spain, when Cardinal Tarancon was very outspoken in denouncing infringements of human rights, and would certainly have been put in prison if the nuncio had not protected and defended him with diplomatic means.

(e) Nowadays there is hardly any persecution of Christians in the traditional sense. No system could afford to do it. Since the Fifties in China Christians are no longer made 'martyrs': they are condemned for 'crimes against the people'. Modern martyrs do not die for an article of faith, for orthodoxy, but for orthopraxy, for acting in the cause of justice, as their faith requires, in their private and public lives. The 'innocent', too, can die as a result of the mass measures of cruel rulers. Such people can rightly be called martyrs. No less a person than Pope John Paul II affirmed this recently on a visit to the Ardeatine mass grave near Rome on 21 March 1982, where on 24 March 1944 335 innocent hostages were shot as a reprisal by the German SS. The pope went on from there to the old catacombs of St Sebastian and declared, 'Here we are in the old catacombs, so near those catacombs of modern times, the Ardeatine mass grave'.

(f) The 'priests and politics' question is still causing some confusion. If the 'commitment to justice is an essential part of evangelisation itself' as the 1971 Synod of Bishops said, the priest cannot be forbidden to take energetic measures on behalf of peace and justice. Yet the pope uses every occasion, in Puebla, in his addresses in Africa, etc., to emphasise that priests should keep out of politics. But one only has to look at his efforts on behalf of Poland to see that he himself is energetically involved in politics. He probably means that the priest should keep out of party politics, should not be identified with any party, since, as an official representative of the Church, he should be above parties, not opposed to any particular group; furthermore, in the service of justice he ought not to use violent means. But this can hardly mean him not taking part in concrete, political and legitimate action. Should the celibate priest only preach and exhort the laity to work for justice, while he keeps out of the way and leaves married laypeople to take all the risks? That would be neither courageous nor evangelical, for the Good Shepherd gives his life for his sheep (John 10:11).

2. CONCRETE SITUATIONS

We shall not be looking back to recent history to analyse the attitude of the institutional Church in the periods of persecution in Mexico 1924-1935, Spain 1931-1939, under Hitler's Nazism and during Stalin's 'Gulag' era. We are restricting ourselves to the present time in the two ideological systems, the Marxist States of the East and the 'national security' States of Latin America. For the persecution of Christians only exists where ideology has the upper hand. The person free from ideology does not persecute others, but pursues dialogue and agreement. According to their horizon and point of view some see modern martyrs primarily in the East, others primarily in Latin America.[4]

(a) The Eastern States

In principle Marxism guarantees the freedom of religion. Even in Lenin's time the following clause was made part of the constitution of the USSR: 'Every person has the right to practise a religion or no religion.' This clause has been incorporated into the constitution of most of the Marxist States, e.g., Mozambique, Angola, Ethiopia. But in practice conditions vary greatly from country to country. The most radical situation is that in Albania, whereas in Hungary conditions are almost normal. In Russia and Czechoslovakia the situation is very close to persecution. Everything is being done to stamp out faith, apart, as a rule, from physical pressure. In Marxist States believers in general are regarded as underdeveloped, backward, third-rate people, still living in superstition, from which they need to be freed through science. Anyone who professes faith cannot be a member of the Party and is often at a disadvantage in public and social life.

In its *Ostpolitik*[5] the Vatican has for decades endeavoured to reach a minimum, through negotiations, which would permit freedom of worship, doctrine and practical living. In all this the Vatican avoids judging these governments morally. It regards them as a *fait accompli* and hopes to be reciprocally recognised. The bishops of these countries for the most part took up a stance of confrontation and were annoyed to find that the Vatican was engaging in 'diplomacy' over their heads. But even in the last years of Paul VI they changed their minds, seeing that more could be achieved by negotiation than by confrontation.

In the example of Poland one can see that the Church is not content merely with the guarantee of freedom of worship; here, as with one voice, the Vatican, the Primate and the Bishops' Conference are demanding freedom for the people to determine their own path. Here it is very evident that the regime is divorced from the people whereas the Church is identified with it. The Church has become the third political power next to the regime and 'Solidarity'. Before General Jaruzelski travelled to Moscow at the end of February 1982 the Bishops' Conference declared, 'We are on the brink of a catastrophe. A solution can only be found through a renewal of dialogue in freedom.' After Easter they published a document towards a settlement of the crisis, in which they stubbornly demanded the release of political prisoners. Here we see a decidedly courageous Church.

(b) In the 'national security' States of Latin America

This ideology affirms that national security is the highest criterion. Everything else, including personal freedom, must be subordinated to it. In practice, however, 'national security' is equated with the maintenance of the existing order, which represents the interests of the ruling class, the government, the military and the large landowners.

Previously the institutional Church itself was part of the regime, but since Medellín in 1968 a change of heart has taken place in many bishops' conferences, and not only among bishops but also among priests and religious. In Poland the bishops represent the Church and the priests simply obey; in Latin America the priests and religious pursue a more independent path.

The great diversity of situations here can be seen from the bishops' conferences of Argentina and of Brazil. In Argentina the bishops are mostly loyal to the government although it is one of those countries where thousands of people simply 'disappear' and the government releases no information about them. In Brazil, by contrast, the bishops' conference has continually represented to the government how the gap between the rich and the poor in this country is getting bigger and bigger. In a recent white paper the bishops have proved, among other things, that between May 1980 and September 1981 thirty-five small farmers were killed by rapacious magnates in conflicts over the possession of land. Archbishop Helder Camara and Cardinal Arns are seen as the strongest representatives of this courageous church. But many other bishops, too, who are concerned about the rights of little people, are said to be 'red'. This was why, years ago, Bishop Adriano Hypolito was abducted, stripped, and left, covered with red paint. Here one can really speak of the persecution of Christians, where people who try to carry out the demands of justice which arise out of faith, suffer torture and death.

The apostolic nuncios in Latin America are mostly regarded as being too conformist, too diplomatic. Here the interplay of prophetic and diplomatic charisma we referred to earlier hardly operates at all. Instead we see a continuation of the tradition in which the Church was generally hard in its attitude to the 'red' Marxists, but gentle in dealing with the 'brown' and 'black' Fascists. It is always inclined to be friendly with 'Catholic' governments,[6] although in actual fact a 'fraternal correction' would be more appropriate here than in the case of atheists.

A dire example was provided by the nuncio to Nicaragua prior to the coup. He was regarded as a friend of President Samoza. But when the bishops produced an incisive pastoral letter saying among other things that the representatives of law and order in that country had become the greatest criminals, far from advising his friend that things were becoming dangerous, that the bishops were complaining, that things must be changed, he angrily told the bishops that they should not have published the letter.

On the other hand the nuncio in Guatemala does not defend the attitude of the Cardinal, who is very pro-government and seems to be saying to the people, 'Be content as long as you have the mass'. Therefore Pope John Paul II himself stepped in and in a letter of 1 November 1980 reminded the entire episcopate of the Church's responsibility to work more diligently and courageously for the good of the people.

In Cuba, finally, the nuncio has maintained good relations with President Fidel Castro, gaining much from him and encouraging the bishops and priests to engage in a critical collaboration with the government. Some denounced him as 'red' but Rome honoured him by nominating him in 1974 as President of the 'Pontificia Academia Ecclesiastica' where the Vatican's future diplomats are trained.

All in all it presents a varied picture. The institutional Church is by no means always as 'one' as people think.

Translated by Graham Harrison

Notes

1. The situation in question is found all over the globe and in very diverse forms. To deal with them would require dozens of monographs. Of necessity this article is general and has few

references. The latter can be found, e.g., in *Documentation catholique*. I have also drawn on conversations with various Vatican representatives, but out of prudence and consideration no names are given here. For further literature see: J. D. Holmes *The Papacy in the modern world* (New York 1981); H. Helbling *Politik der Päpste. Der Vatikan im Weltgeschehen 1958-1978* (Frankfurt a.M 1981); *Agostino Kardinal Casaroli: Der Heilige Stuhl und die Völkergemeinschaft* ed. H. Schambeck (Berlin 1981).

2. See the classical texts in *Gaudium et Spes*, §44, footnote 148 (in the edition by Walter Abbot).

3. See W. Bühlmann *Die Lehren aus der Ketzergeschichte* (Zurich 1982).

4. See two typical books: G. Hamburger *Verfolgte Christen. Berichte aus unserer Zeit* (Graz 1979) and M. Lange/R. Iblacker *Christenverfolgung in Südamerika* (Freiburg i.B. 1980).

5. See H. J. Stehle *Die Ostpolitik des Vatikans* (Munich 1975).

6. Something similar was evident in the colonisation period in the second half of the last century. The Vatican never reacted against Catholic King Leopold's conquest of the Congo, in part a very cruel one, whereas it roundly condemned the conquest of Eritrea by the liberal and anti-Church Italy, threatening those responsible with the judgment of God. This did not occur, however, in the case of the conquest of Abyssinia by Mussolini, who was well-disposed towards the Church. See P. Grossrieder *Le Saint Siège et la colonisation en Afrique Centrale au 19ème siècle* (Fribourg 1982).

Desmond Tutu

Persecution of Christians Under Apartheid

1. INTRODUCTION

A FEW days before I sat down to write this piece something happened which is germane to this paper. A car belonging to Dr Beyers Naude, the banned Director of the now proscribed Christian Institute of South Africa was set ablaze by a bomb which the police later described as the work of an expert in explosives. The fire was put out without much damage to life or property as it happened when the car was standing out in a yard where it was being serviced and the quick thinking and quick action of the man in whose yard it was standing prevented further damage. But supposing the bomb had exploded a little earlier or a little later—would be be telling the same fairly mild story of anonymous terrorist activity—supposing it had gone off whilst Dr Beyers Naude or his wife, Ilse, had been driving it, would we not today be speaking about a real blood martyr or martyrs? But that is to go ahead of my story somewhat.

The incident itself was a good illustration of the two types of persecution of Christians that are possible and do occur under apartheid. One could say that the one form of persecution is by direct action of the government which takes different shapes—and the five-year ban on Dr Naude is an example of such persecution—about this more a little later. The second type can be described as due to what could be called popular action from a certain constituency supportive of the government or even more extreme policies than those of the government and who are not averse from taking the law (such as it is in our beloved land) into their own hands and making life difficult and for some people literally impossible as in the case of assassinations. This kind of persecution is usually the handiwork of so-called right-wing groups.

1. SUFFERING AND THE CHRISTIAN: AN IMPORTANT CAVEAT

Before we consider specific examples of the two main broad types of persecution that have happened and still happen under apartheid it is necessary to place an important caveat. Christians have no right to be surprised when they suffer and are persecuted for witnessing to the love and justice and righteousness of God and of his Son Jesus Christ our Lord. The point is that our Lord and Master made it quite clear that suffering for the sake of the Name was not to be regarded as something peculiar and out of the ordinary. No, on the contrary it was constitutive of being a Christian. He pronounced a special beatitude on those who were persecuted for righteousness' sake for they would be rewarded—theirs would be the Kingdom of Heaven. They would be particularly blessed for suffering insults and persecution and all kinds of calumny for His sake. These were to be accepted with gladness and exultation for their reward would be rich in Heaven. They must bear in mind that such was the persecution which was visited on the prophets of old (Matt. 5:10-12).

Even if we make allowance for the peculiar *Sitz in Leben* or context of a fair proportion of the New Testament which would colour the dominical and other material preserved in it, we must nonetheless acknowledge that our Lord appeared to expect that Christianity and suffering were not alien to and inconsistent with one another. In another part of the New Testament, Christians are exhorted to bear their suffering with dignity and forebearance because they were following in the footsteps of one who had himself suffered. 'Jesus Christ suffered for you, leaving you an example, that you should follow in his footsteps. He committed no sin, no guile was found on his lips; when he was reviled, he did not revile in return. When he suffered, he did not threaten, but trusted in him who judges justly' (1 Pet. 2:21-23).

We should not be like Peter who, appalled at the prospect of a suffering and dying Messiah, remonstrated with the Lord whose Messiahship he had just confessed and for which he had been so specially felicitated (Matt. 16:13-23). We should recall that the Lord went on thereafter to describe the nature of true discipleship: 'If anyone wishes to be a follower of mine; he must leave self behind; he must take up his cross and come with me' (Matt. 16:24). He is quite categorical, that unless we take up our cross and follow him, we cannot be his disciples (Luke 14:26 ff.). He warns that the world hated him and therefore it should come as no surprise that it hates us who are his followers. If it had loved him then presumably it would have loved his followers as well.

2. TEST OF AUTHENTICITY

In many ways, Jesus declares, the attitude of the world and its authorities will help to determine his true followers. That treatment will be one of the criteria to help distinguish the true from the false Church (John 15:18-21). Consequently, we must not be taken aback at suffering and persecution which come our way. In many ways what Shylock in *The Merchant of Venice* said of Jews, should be applied more aptly to the Christians—'Suffering is the badge of all our tribe'. In my view, since the cross is so central to the life and work of Jesus Christ and makes him into the sort of Saviour he is for this sort of world, the cross and suffering must be central also to the life and work of the Christian.

If this is so and Scripture seems to declare that it is so (Paul for instance declares that we can participate in the glory of the Resurrection only if we share in his suffering and death), then it must mean that surprise must be occasioned for the Christian not by suffering and persecution but by their absence. A Christian or a Church that does not suffer is a contradiction in terms. It is as meaningless and ridiculous as a Christ without the passion and death. A crossless Christ could not have been the Saviour of the world. A Church that does not suffer cannot be the Church of Jesus Christ of Nazareth who was given up into the hands of wicked men and who suffered, died and was buried. Because if he did not die then he could not have been raised. There could have been no Easter Day unless there had been a Good Friday first. There could have been no Resurrection unless there had been a crucifixion (Rom. 8:17-18). We must remember that our Lord said that unless a grain of wheat falls to the ground and dies, it remains alone: but if it falls to the ground and does die then that is how it will germinate and sprout and grow into a plant (John 12:23-26). The Christian Church is a suffering and dying community for only so can it be a forgiving Community of the Resurrection.

When a church suffers, fellow Christians elsewhere should not mourn as if something were happening that was foreign to the nature of the Church, something totally surprising catching us off balance. No, we should rejoice as the Apostles of our Lord rejoiced: 'They sent for the Apostles and had them flogged; then they ordered them to give up speaking in the name of Jesus and discharged them. So the Apostles went from the Council rejoicing that they had been found worthy to suffer indignity for the sake of the Name. And every day they went steadily on with their teaching in the temple and in private houses, telling the good news of Jesus the Messiah.' When Christians are called to suffer for the Name, it is cause for pride—a proper pride in those who are so called and rejoicing in the rest of the Church that their brothers and sisters have been thought worthy of suffering for the blessed Name (Acts 5:40-42).

Yes, we want to be prayed for and supported by our brothers and sisters in other parts of the world, they who are fellow members in the Body of our Lord Jesus Christ and we use Paul's words as most fitting: 'Praise be to the God and Father of our Lord Jesus Christ, the all-Merciful Father, the God whose consolation never fails us! He comforts us in all our troubles, so that we in turn may be able to comfort others in any trouble of theirs and to share with them the consolation we ourselves receive from God. As Christ's cup of suffering overflows, and we suffer with him, so also through Christ our consolation overflows. If distress be our lot, it is the price we pay for your consolation, for your salvation; if our lot be consolation, it is to help us to bring you comfort, and strength to face with fortitude the same sufferings we now endure. And our hope for you is firmly grounded; for we know that if you have part in the suffering, you have part also in the divine consolation.' 'This was meant to teach us not to place reliance on ourselves, but on God who raises the dead. From such mortal peril God delivered us; and he will deliver us again, he on whom our hope is fixed. Yes, he will continue to deliver us, if you will co-operate by praying for us. Then, with so many people praying for our deliverance, there will be many to give thanks on our behalf for the gracious favour God has shown towards us.' (2 Cor. 1:3-7, 9-11).

That is how the tables are turned on the devil just at the point of what he would consider his triumph. I find I am attracted more and more to the vision of the souls under the altar in the book of the Revelation of St John the divine, who long for the consummation which will bring their vindication after being slaughtered for God's word and for their testimony. They cry out 'How long, sovereign Lord, holy and true, must it be before thou wilt vindicate us and avenge our blood on the inhabitants of the earth?'. The amazing answer they get is not that things will be all right soon. No, they are told to wait a little while longer, until the tally should be complete of all their brothers in Christ who were to be killed as they had been. Liberation and freedom as well as true reconciliation and peace will forever be costly.

We are all called to suffer and to die in Christ's name so that we may live with his resurrection life.

3. PERSECUTION

Many people find it strange that Christians should speak of their persecution in South Africa when the South African government is at pains to proclaim its Christianity. Such people will refer to the fact that there is freedom of worship in this land, that Sunday is observed religiously with a sabbatarian strictness, gambling, casinos and blue films are not allowed. How can anybody speak seriously of the persecution of Christians for being Christian? Unfortunately, we *can* speak about the persecution of Christians by fellow Christians in government and the major reason is that those in power resent being hauled over the coals by those who do so from a Christian perspective in articulating their abhorrence for and opposition to the official policies of the South African government.

These policies are based on the racist ideology of apartheid (a word that has rightly gained the South African Nationalist government nearly universal disapproval) which says the most important fact about any human being is the colour of his skin which is used to determine where one is born (a Black ghetto or a salubrious White segregated residential), where one is educated (with segregated education and institutions), what jobs one can do and what wages one earns, how freely one can move, whom one can marry and eventually where one will be buried (for in death as well the races must be kept rigidly apart in their own separate cemeteries). The ideology is designed to keep power and privilege in the hands of the White minority with a plethora of racist and Draconian legislation, much of which would be the envy of many a totalitarian and un-Christian State. Apartheid has caused untold misery to many millions of God's children whose value as those created in the image of God is denied and whose human dignity has been trampled underfoot. The victims of apartheid are legion. It is the mother and her children left behind in the unviable Bantustan homeland to eke out a miserable existence whilst father and husband goes to the 'white' man's town to work as a migrant labourer living in a single-sex hostel for eleven months of the year—this migratory labour system effectively destroying Black family life. Among these victims are the several millions who have been uprooted from their former homes in what have become Black spots in White areas and who have been dumped in the Bantustan ghettos of misery and inexhaustible reservoirs of cheap labour. If and when Christians have opposed these vicious laws and the unjust socio-political and economic structures of South African society then they have come up against the might of the South African authorities who have become increasingly intolerant of debate, discussion and dissent, as the spate of new laws show to control the dissemination of information and the press. Such persons also run the gauntlet of popular White hostility which could break out into horrendous expression of a nasty kind.

Our survey of persecution goes back to the decade of the 1950s when the repression was just starting and apartheid was just getting under way. The stalwarts we have in mind were Christians of the stature and calibre of a Michael Scott, the Anglican priest who protested against slum housing in what was to become Soweto near Johannesburg by staying in a tent and sharing those ghetto conditions with Blacks and was arrested for his Christian witness. We think with pride of such as Trevor Huddleston, CR, now Anglican Archbishop of the Indian Ocean, who had won the hearts of many struggling for justice in South Africa but especially the hearts of Blacks whose cause he espoused with such concerned Christian zeal and passion. He protested against the demolition of Sophiatown, a suburb of Johannesburg, where Blacks had freehold tenure and their removal under Dr Verwoerd's Black spots edict to Soweto where they could only rent their matchbox houses. He was active also in the human rights movement and shared in the historic meeting at Kliptown when the Freedom Charter was signed in 1955. His Community recalled him to England, many believed because he might soon bear the brunt of government action.

4. DIRECT STATE ACTION TO REPRESS DISSENT

The Nationalist government was quite unmoved by the Passive Resistance campaign of 1952 organised by the African National Congress. Based on the methods of Mahatma

Gandhi it sought the abolition of repressive legislation such as the Pass Laws which apply only to Blacks and severely restrict their right to move freely in the land of their birth. The government responded harshly to these attempts at peaceful non-coöperation with apartheid culminating in the brutal action of the police at Sharpeville in 1960 when the South African police opened fire on Blacks demonstrating peacefully against the Pass Laws. A State of Emergency was declared early that year, and people such as Robert Mangaliso Sobukwe were arrested for being opposed to the apartheid laws. He was a gentle, peace-loving University teacher and a devout lay preacher in the Methodist Church. He served his sentence in the maximum security prison on Robben Island. After his sentence had been served, he was kept on Robben Island by special legislation. On his release he was restricted with a banning order to Kimberley where he was later to die of cancer. The apartheid regime had treated the outstanding Christian leader of the ANC, Chief Albert Luthuli, Nobel Peace Prize winner, in the same way. He was restricted to a rural area in Natal serving a banning order. Such an order, usually lasting five years and renewable, condemns persons to a twilight existence as non-persons. They must remain within a prescribed area leaving it only with permission seldom given. They cannot be quoted, cannot attend gatherings (either social or political) and a gathering is more than two people. Banning is a convenient way of punishing an opponent because it is a purely arbitrary bureaucratic act by a government minister without recourse to the courts of law to test the evidence allegedly justifying the ban. The African National Congress and the Pan-African Congress to which many Black Christians belonged were banned, denying thousands the means of expressing their grievances, hopes and aspirations through democratic organs. Many Christians were amongst the accused in the Treason Trial (1956-1961) in which all were later acquitted.

In the aftermath of Sharpeville, the South African Government deported the outspoken Anglican Bishop of Johannesburg Ambrose Reeves. This action signalled a tightening of the screws of repression especially on the critics of apartheid most of whom, as we have pointed out, were Christians constrained by the imperatives of the Gospel of Jesus Christ to speak out against injustice and oppression. The government had laws such as the Suppression of Communism Act which ironically was being used ruthlessly against committed Christians to silence them with banning orders. There were laws providing for detention without trial, precursors of the more notorious Section 6 of the Terrorism Act under which the authorities could hold detainees incommunicado in solitary confinement indefinitely, without benefit of due judicial process. Medical evidence has shown that solitary confinement itself is a form of torture, apart from the allegations of police brutality against the detainees. Forty-six persons are *known* to have died mysteriously during detention. One of the more well-known of these was Steve Biko—a committed Christian seeking a new, a more just, a more democratic non-racial South Africa. The world was stunned at what he suffered as revealed in the inquest and was shocked by his callous death. Is he is Christian martyr—are the many Christians who have died in detention and in other ways in the liberation struggle Christian martyrs?

Several Christians have been detained without trial for lengthy periods. Thom Manthata, an SACC (South African Council of Churches) worker, has been in and out of jail several times, once spending a total of 230 days in solitary confinement, then nearly a year in preventive detention but never charged even once; Mrs Sally Motlana, Vice-President of the SACC, has had at least two periods of solitary confinement without trial; the Rev. Sol Jacob, working on the issue of South African refugees for the SACC, was detained for nearly two months last year in solitary confinement; Mrs Bernadette Mosala, also of the SACC, has had a spell of solitary confinement as have SACC field workers in other parts of the country. Fr. Smangaliso Mkhatswa, Secretary

General of the South African Catholic Bishops' Conference, languished in jail in preventive detention and is now enduring a second five-year banning order. Alexander Mbatha, a field worker for the SACBC, and his wife spent nearly three months in detention without trial. Sometimes the authorities might try to get at you through your children. Duma, the seventeen-year-old son of the Methodist President Dr Simon Gqubule (also Vice-President of the SACC), is currently experiencing his second spell in detention in solitary confinement. The Rev. Frank Chikane of the Apostolic Faith Mission has been in detention now for months on end. Several Lutheran pastors were held in detention in Vendaland, a spuriously independent Bantustan, for several months and they claim to have been tortured. The State then withdrew the charges it brought against them. They are victims of apartheid because the Bantustans are South Africa's client States—the appendages of apartheid. Many Christians have suffered the wrath of the South African Government in the form of passport refusals, others being unable to take up necessary work in South Africa because visas and work permits have been refused. A second Anglican Bishop of Kimberley and Kuruman, Graham Chadwick, has been drummed out of the RSA largely we believe for helping people facing political charges. Now he lives in Bophutatswana. If we added Namibia, then the catalogue of woe is lengthened almost interminably—three Anglican bishops have been expelled from that territory, the most well known being Colin Winter who recently died soon after relinquishing his job as Bishop in exile. Many other church workers have suffered the same fate of deportation from Namibia. Annoyed by the freedom on the campus of the Federal Theological Seminary which existed cheek by jowl with the Black apartheid University of Fort Hare, the government offered to buy the Fedsem ostensibly to provide land for Fort Hare's expansion. When the Fedsem rejected the offer, the government exercised its powers by expropriating this ecumenical institution despite previous assurances of its security of tenure.

The government uses Commissions of Inquiry to prepare the way for its repressive action against certain individuals and organisations. It used the Schlebusch Commission to act against the renowned Christian Institute founded and led by the redoubtable Beyers Naude who with some of his colleagues had a five-year ban slapped on him. The Christian Institute was closed down and its periodical *Pro Veritate* was proscribed. The government has recently appointed the Eloff Judicial Commission to investigate the SACC and if they are true to form, they are surely going to take drastic action against that body. They have already twice removed the passport of its General Secretary as a punitive measure because they do not like what he said whilst overseas.

We must include in direct government action of persecuting Christians, the treatment that is meted out to conscientious objectors who are subjected to long terms of imprisonment in detention barracks even, as in the case of Charles Yates, when the military tribunal is impressed with the sincerity of their Christian convictions.

5. POPULAR ACTION

Many Christians are the objects of ridicule, vilification and worse at the hands of the public. Often it is the same people who are already being persecuted by the State with banning orders, etc., who are the target of this hostility from sections of the White community. We have referred to what happened to the car of Beyers Naude. He and others like himself perceived as 'enemies of the people' receive abusive and threatening telephone calls, have delivered to their homes goods such as lorryloads of sand or trucks of liquor that they have not ordered. Their lives are threatened by extreme right-wing groups such as the Wit Kommando; pot-shots are taken at them. They live under the threat of physical violence and are often exposed to character assassination in the media especially SABC TV and Radio, really no more than a propaganda tool for the government, with no right to reply. The Info Scandal of 1980 showed that the authorities will stop at nothing to get at their opponents. The right-wing Christian League of Southern Africa was used to undermine the SACC and nobody has yet apologised. For those opposed to apartheid as Christians, it is often as if we live not in a country claiming to be Christian but in a country behind the Iron Curtain, with plot and counter-plot. Scurrilous pamphlets have sometimes been distributed to discredit apartheid's critics as well.

6. CONCLUSION

The Christian victims of apartheid remain true to the best tradition of those who have suffered for Christ. Thom Manthata, after being released from preventive detention, said, 'Thank you for praying for us. Let us not be consumed by hate or bitterness.' Malusi Mpumlwana having been banned with his young wife, on release from detention said about his White police torturers, 'As they torture you, you think "These are God's children and they are behaving like animals. They need us to help them recover the humanity they have lost."' God be praised.

This incomplete catalogue of repression is depressing. The government are ruthless and vicious and will put down opposition without compunction and any scruple. Some people have died mysteriously in what have been brutal assassinations. The Black community has no doubt about the identity of the culprits. Apartheid is producing Christian martyrs (both white and red martyrs). Evil seems rampant and good has its nose rubbed in the dust.

'With all this in mind, what are we to say? If God is on our side, who is against us?'

'Then what can separate us from the love of Christ? Can affliction or hardship? Can persecution, hunger, nakedness, peril, or the sword? "We are being done to death for thy sake all day long", as Scripture says; "we have been treated like sheep for slaughter"—and yet, in spite of all, overwhelming victory is ours through him who loved us. For I am convinced that there is nothing in death or life, in the realm of spirits or superhuman powers, in the world as it is or the world as it shall be, in the forces of the universe, in heights or depths—nothing in all creation that can separate us from the love of God in Christ Jesus our Lord.' (Romans 8:31, 35-39).

Abel Herzberg

Did the Holocaust of the Jews Count as Martyrdom?

THE FOLLOWING article looks at the notion of martyrdom. Is it applicable outside the Church when the Church has had a hand in the historical process? Were the Jews, killed in Auschwitz, simply victims or martyrs, or perhaps both? Were there signs of God's presence in Auschwitz?

I am a Jew, born of Russian parents in Amsterdam in 1893. I took a degree in law, married, with three children, and functioned as a lawyer from 1925 till 1980, except from March 1943 till April 1945, when I was interned in various camps by the Germans who had occupied Holland, for the last fifteen months with my wife—the youngsters had gone 'underground'.

It is thus as a Jew that I am contributing some thoughts on the subject the Editor invited me to write about.

I did not, however, accept without some hesitation. This is because I think and move in secular terms while 'martyrdom' is above all a concept with religious implications. But this hesitation vanished when I realised that a martyr is not exclusively somebody who is persecuted because of his idea of God or his behaviour in so far as it is based on this, and yet refuses to change his mind. He may support or even be actively committed to some other cause which is noble, at least in his own eyes, and to which he will remain committed in spite of all suffering and not infrequently even death. I take it for granted, of course, that both men and women can be martyrs. But the victim of sheer persecution is a different proposition. I mean that while a martyr can certainly be described as a victim, not every victim is a martyr—far from it.

The *martyr* has chosen his own conviction, has freely chosen to live accordingly, and in any case represents it. The *victim* may be condemned or forced to lead a diminished existence without any personal choice or provocation. The victim has far more sense of having been hit by misfortune than of having to obey a call.

Let us have a look at which of the two categories would fit the Jews who were caught up in the holocaust. This is also important because, essentially, all Jews in the world are involved in this holocaust event. Many are clearly directly linked with it. All the others cannot escape a sense of solidarity with those that actually were exterminated. This sense of solidarity is both felt by the Jews themselves, and attributed to them by general opinion. No Jew has been able to ignore the holocaust. Perhaps one may say that every Jew in the world, even though he has survived the event, like the author of this article,

70

carries the scar of the holocaust. This remark does not only apply to the holocaust. There has been no Jewish persecution in history which did not have more or less the same effect. One might even say that this scar is the most distinctive mark of the Jew today. And even if it is not always observable, it is always there.

No Jew was seen as a martyr in the holocaust. He was not even granted that honour. He was simply a victim, had to remain a victim and nothing beyond that. Obviously the Jew was persecuted, robbed, tortured and killed solely as a Jew. But the decisive issue is whether we should see all this misery as mere persecution or as martyrdom in the case of the Jew as such? So, who was this Jew of the holocaust?

He was not seen as a fellow human who had witnessed to and experienced God and his oneness in his own way. So he was not seen as representing a religious tradition with which he had been identified for centuries. This is already ruled out because most of those Jews had already abandoned this tradition for decades but were not exempted from this holocaust. Nor was there any distinctive psychological or intellectual slant which the oppressor could use to justify the proposed extermination of all those who, in his eyes, were 'Jews'. It proved also impossible to find any distinctive bodily feature which, according to the oppressor, marked all those who had no right to exist. Nor could he damn the whole lot of those Jews because of any social or political solidarity.

All the same, there had to be some criterion by which to judge who should die and who should not. In the gamut of arguments there was nothing left but the naked fact of a person's birth. And so they came to invent the Jewish race.

It did not exist. It was a fiction. A thing like a 'race', let alone a pure and exclusive race, and on top of that a 'Jewish' one, could not even exist. But this made no difference.

The fact is that Germany had been humiliated. It was poor and, through the Treaty of Versailles, was overwhelmed by all kinds of problems. It had to regain its honour and power. This led to the urge to dominate Europe and even other continents. Hegemony was the basic motivation.

None of this could be achieved without war, so war was necessary. The amount of blood and misery it would cost was considered irrelevant. The overriding requirement was armament to the teeth and the mobilisation of all the material resources which were available. And this requirement was turned into the primary duty of all Germans. But in order to meet this problem it was vital to prepare for the strategic mobilisation by a campaign which would psychologically condition people to go along with it. This means that no people in the world will go to war without being shown the enemy to be destroyed in the flesh.

This 'conditioning' mobilisation took the line of an unlimited hatred of Jews and so the enemy picked out to be destroyed became Jewry at large. It could hardly be otherwise. For who in the world had been a threat to the German people before Adolf Hitler seized power, and even after that, before the Second World War? Like every other nation Germany had its competitors but none of them could be described as enemies. To a large extent one might even maintain the opposite. Only one has to think of the rather extensive concessions made by Chamberlain to Hitler in Munich, concessions which were at the time applauded by a large majority of citizens in a number of countries. Did not even Stalin, in spite of his distaste for Fascism in principle, conclude a pact with its 'Führer'?

As I said, Hitler needed a war. But it is hard to fight a war if you have no enemy. So, where do you look for one? In history of course. There one finds largely dormant instincts which can be re-kindled into new fires. There is no doubt that Hitler had an aversion to Jews. That is why he could not do without them. He admitted this himself. One of his most remembered *dicta* was: 'If the Jews didn't exist we would have to invent them.' What he did not say was that he actually did invent them. They did not exist, at least certainly not in the way he drew up their public 'image', which was as the principal, and indeed the only real target for the Germanic nations.

History provides more than enough evidence for persecutions of the Jews. And here the churches can hardly be said not to have done their bit. Hitler was aware of those persecutions, actually referred to them, but mainly to stress the fact that they did not go far enough. He found them too sentimentally influenced, too one-sided, too limited in approach. The reason was that in the past the Jews were accused of this or that mental attitude, thought to be pernicious, or of this or that objectionable misdemeanour. But he, the great architect of a new and clean world, had found out that they were the carriers of bacilli which infect life on this earth and that of all mankind.

This is why they should not be condemned for one particular crime, however serious, nor for any particular opinion, however abominable, but simply because they were there, they existed. It was because of this very existence which in its malign nature aimed at world domination that they had to be liquidated. In his ideology Hitler called this 'concentrating on an opponent'; in practice it became his 'final solution of the Jewish question' (*Endlösung der Judenfrage*). One of the places where the execution had to take place was Auschwitz. I have never been there. I had the advantage of being put away in Bergen Belsen—and it was an advantage, although in a very relative sense.

Auschwitz was a 'Vernichtungslager', i.e., an extermination camp, which meant that none of its prisoners was ever allowed to leave the camp alive. Bergen Belsen, on the other hand, was a kind of *dépôt* for a number of Jews who were destined to be exchanged for 'Reichsdeutsche' (Nazi citizens) when an opportunity occurred. Although this exchange indeed took place on rare occasions, it was an illusion for the majority of them. These Jews were there long enough to acquire a thorough understanding of what the 'final solution' actually meant. It is obvious that what was experienced there was equally valid, at least in principle, for the situation in other camps, including Auschwitz.

The first thing one realised was that there was no point in imagining that one was a martyr for a good cause, which one had to uphold or for which one had to endure all kinds of torments. One was not persecuted for what one was but for what one was not and therefore fought. One was simply a reject, nothing more. One was condemned to be a mere reject, the mere scum of humanity, and that constituted one's daily experience of actual reality.

In any case, who can think in terms of 'martyrdom' when you see small children perishing in concentration camps? You can only be a 'martyr' when you have reached the age of understanding, and who would expect this sort of understanding in children? So we have all been victims—let us leave it at that.

But this in no sense means that God was not present in Bergen Belsen, which is no doubt also true for Auschwitz and other camps.

So I have seen old people die who had a desperate longing to see their children before the end. But when they realised that this was an illusion they accepted the fact and left this earthly existence with the Jewish belief in the oneness of God on their parched lips. Innumerable people, starved and martyred in the concentration camps, thus abandoned this earthly life, even while they were being gassed. Lone rebels among the faithful accused God, on whom they had based their whole existence, of injustice because he allowed what in fact happened. Yet, rebellion can just as validly be an expression of the experience of God as humility. As a poet put it:

When I fly from Thee, my God,
To whom shall I turn,
If not to Thee?

In hours that were really wasted I secretly observed feasts which were loaded with traditional Blessings at the Jewish New Year; others full of gratitude for the delivery from the slavery of Egypt, never so keenly experienced as in the even harsher slavery which beset the participants, in tears, yet, full of joy about the law given in the Sinai desert, and full of hope for the restoration of Israel in freedom and independence.

A woman who was persecuted once told me that Hitler had violated man as the image of God.

Was all this not perhaps the last and most profound reply to the holocaust with its swastika, and indeed its direct opposite? The rejecting of rejection, a return to some of the noblest values in human civilisation, an awareness of sharing in these values in spite of all the hunger and misery?

And, with all this in mind, are we not entitled here to speak of persevering unto death in clinging to a personal truth, the kind of perseverance which led so many martyrs to their death?

Translated by T. L. Westow

F

James Cone

Martin Luther King: The Source for His Courage to Face Death

NOT MUCH has been written about Martin Luther King, Jr., and the relation of his theology to the Black Church. Many persons assume that the Black Church made no decisive impact upon King's intellectual life. To explain his theology, most interpreters turn to his teachers at Crozer Theological Seminary and Boston University.[1] The implication of this procedure is that King's theological perspective was defined exclusively by the intellectual impact of White western theology and philosophy and not by the Black Church. While I do not deny the influence of his seminary and university teachers, yet I do think that the influence of the Black Church was much more decisive in shaping his theological perspective.

I contend that the source for King's courage to face death, from Montgomery (1955) to Memphis (1968), was the faith and theology of the Black Church. The primary purpose of this essay is to demonstrate that point.

1. THE BLACK CHURCH AND MARTIN LUTHER KING

Martin King was a product of the Black Church. When the question is asked, 'Who is Martin King?' or 'What is his theology?' neither question can be answered properly without giving major attention to the context of King's origin in the Black Church.

Martin King was the son of a Baptist preacher, and he entered the ministry during his student years at Morehouse College. While he was deeply influenced by his teachers at Crozer Theological Seminary and Boston University, the Black Church was much more decisive in determining his theology, even though King seldom referred to it when he attempted to explain the course of his intellectual development. When asked about the sources of his theological perspective, Martin King referred to such persons as Henry David Thoreau, Mahatma Gandhi, Reinhold Niebuhr, Walter Rauschenbusch, L. Harold De Wolf, and Edgar Sheffield Brightman. I think it is unquestionably true that these philosophers and theologians, as well as other writers and teachers whom King encountered in graduate school, had a profound effect upon the content, shape, and depth of his theological perspective. They provided the intellectual structure for him to express his ideas about love, non-violence, the value of the human person, and the existence of a moral order in the universe. When King was asked to give an explanation

74

for an action or belief, the question usually came from the White community, and he almost always answered the question by appealing to intellectual sources that were regarded as persuasive authorities in the community from which the questions were derived. Martin King seldom had to defend his perspective to Black people, and when he was required, as with the advocates of Black Power,[2] White intellectual resources were never mentioned, because that would have been a sure way to lose the argument. The references to the intellectual tradition of western philosophy and theology are primarily for the benefit of the White public so that King could demonstrate to them that he could think as well or better than any other seminary or university graduate. Furthermore King knew that he could not receive substantial support from the White community until he explained to their satisfaction what he believed and why. If he had appealed directly to the Black Church tradition as the primary source of this theological and political perspective, no one in the White community would have taken him seriously, since the Black Church is usually not thought of as being the origin of intellectual ideas regarding theology or social change.

But I contend that King's failure to refer directly to the Black Church as the chief source for his theological perspective does not mean that it is not, in fact, the primary source. What then is the evidence for my claim regarding the primacy of the Black Church in Martin King's theology? It is difficult to answer this question, because we are accustomed to looking for evidence in printed sources and also from people who knew him personally. While the evidence for my claim does not necessarily contradict what King said about himself or what others say about him, it is not primarily dependent upon their testimonies. My evidence is indirect, and it can only be understood by people who believe that there is an interplay between a person's social context and the ideas he or she promotes. To contend that King's graduate teachers and the books he read in graduate school accounted for the whole of his theological perspective is to discount completely King's early home and church context and thereby suggest that he arrived at Crozer and Boston with a blank mind. Even if we do not hold with Karl Marx's contention that 'consciousness is from the beginning a social product', we cannot claim the opposite, i.e., that 'life is determined by consciousness', and still appropriately account for the whole of a person's perspective. We must say with Marx 'that circumstances make men just as men make circumstances'.[3] If circumstances are relevant in the assessment of a person's ideas and actions, we must then inquire about Martin King's circumstances so that we can understand properly the distinctive contribution of his theology. Using Boston University and Crozer Theological Seminary as the primary resources for understanding King's ideas and actions ignores the enormous impact of the Black Church upon his life and thought. It is like using the theology of John Wesley as the primary determinant for explaining who Richard Allen was, and why he founded the African Methodist Episcopal Church in 1816. We know that such an explanation may be useful in dialogue with White United Methodists or British Methodists but not in explaining the historical and theological significance of Richard Allen or of the church he founded. To understand Richard Allen and the significance of his church, it is necessary to know something of his slave circumstances, and what that meant for African people in North America during the late eighteenth and early nineteenth centuries.[4]

A similar observation can and should be made regarding Martin King's theology. What were the circumstances that determined the perspective of his theology and politics? I contend that the most significant circumstances that shaped King's theology were the oppression of Black people and the liberating message of the Black Church. These two realities—the oppression of Blacks and the Black Church's liberating message of the Gospel—provided King with the intellectual challenge to develop a theology that was Christian and also relevant for the social and political needs of Black people. That was why he entered the ministry while a student at Morehouse and later accepted a call to be pastor of Dexter Avenue Baptist Church in Montgomery, rather than seeking a teaching post at a White seminary or university. In fact King turned down many teaching offers at major White universities and seminaries, and he also refused several invitations to pastor White churches, because of his primary commitment to the Black Church and its message of liberation for Black people.

The Black Church was also the context out of which Martin King accepted the call to be the leader of the Montgomery bus boycott. After his success in Montgomery, King founded the Southern Christian Leadership Conference (SCLC) which received its support primarily from Black preachers and their churches. In order to keep his identity firmly tied to the Black Church as he served as the president of SCLC, he became the co-pastor of Ebenezer Baptist Church in Atlanta. Martin King's close ties with the Black Church in preference over other alternatives indicate that his primary commitment was to that community. Anyone, therefore, who wishes to understand properly his life and thought must make the Black Church the primary source for the analysis.

The best way of deciding what was primary for King's life and thought is to ask, 'What tradition did King turn to in moments of crisis during his ministry?'. Where one turns when one's back is up against the wall, and when everything seems hopeless will tell us far more about his or her theology than what is often printed in articles and books. When King encountered the harsh contradictions of White violence, and when he had run out of rational alternatives on how best to defeat it non-violently, where did he turn for insight, courage, and the hope that things can and will be otherwise? Did he turn to Brightman, DeWolf, Niebuhr, or Gandhi? Of course not! None of these intellectual resources were useful to him in the context of crisis. In moments of crisis when despair was about to destroy the possibility of making a new future for the poor, King turned to the faith contained in the tradition of the Black Church. Whether one speaks of Montgomery, Albany, Birmingham, Selma, Chicago, or Memphis, the crises arising from his struggle to implement justice never produced despair in his theological and political consciousness. The reason is not found in his intellectual grasp and exposition of White liberal theology but in the faith and life of the Black Church. With the resources of this religious tradition, King had a foundation that could sustain him, even though he knew that his struggle for justice would lead to his own death. Publicly and privately with his family and SCLC colleagues, Martin King often spoke of the imminent possibility of his own death. He not only frequently received threats against his life, King also realised that any Black person who dared to challenge the White power structure (especially in the southern part of the US) was risking his life. During the Albany Movement (1961) he said, 'It may get me crucified. I may die. But I want it said even if I die in the struggle that "He died to make me free".'[5] Earlier during the Montgomery bus boycott (1956) he had suggested that 'Once more it might well turn out that the blood of the martyr will be the seed of the tabernacle of freedom'.[6] However, by the time of the Selma March (1965), several persons had died in the struggle of freedom, and thus King told his followers:

> I can't promise you that it won't get you beaten. I can't promise you that it won't get your home bombed. I can't promise you won't get scarred up a bit—but we must stand up for what is right. If you haven't discovered something that is worth dying for, you haven't found anything worth living for.[7]

It is one thing to talk about martyrdom in a university or seminary classroom, but quite another to make a political commitment for others which one knows will lead to death. To understand why and how Martin King could make such a radical commitment, it is necessary to know something about Black people's nearly 400 years of struggle. Martin King comes from a Black religious tradition that empowers Black

Christians to 'Keep on keeping on' even though the odds might be against them. This is the context for understanding the often heard faith claim, 'I ain't no ways tired'. This affirmation of faith is not derived from the faith of middle-class Blacks or Whites and their capitalistic orientation. Rather this faith is derived from the meeting of God in the pains and struggles of poor Blacks who refuse to accept despair as the logical consequence of their oppression, because they firmly believe that 'God can make a way out of no way'. It was Martin King's identity with the tradition of this Black faith that enabled him to overcome crisis moments during his fight for justice. While he was not always sure how to make this faith intellectually convincing to his friends and supporters in the White community, he knew that his own people were already aware of the inability of White concepts to explain the certainty of Black faith. That was why it was so easy for him to get a little carried away when speaking in a Black church. Their enthusiastic responses to his sermons on justice and non-violence, saying 'Amen!', 'Right-on!', 'Speak the truth!', let him know that they were in solidarity with him, and that they would follow him wherever he led them. They had already demonstrated their presence with him in Civil Rights Movements in Montgomery, Birmingham, and Selma. Furthermore, King also knew that their belief in him was in no way dependent upon his theological perspective as defined by White theological resources. Black people followed King, because he embodied in word and deed the faith of the Black Church which has always claimed that oppression and the Gospel of Jesus do not go together.

2. MARTIN KING AND THE ESCHATOLOGY OF THE BLACK CHURCH

What was the main content of King's thought which he derived from the Black Church tradition? This question is not easy to answer because the Black Church has not done much systematic reflection in the area of theology. Our theologies have been presented in the forms of sermons, songs, prayers, testimonies, and stories of slavery and oppression. In these sources we have given our views of God, humanity, and the world, and how each may be understood in relation to our struggle for freedom. We did not write essays on Christian doctrine, because our ancestors came as slaves from Africa and not as free people from Europe. Many Blacks were prevented from learning to read and write either by the circumstances of our birth or by the legal restrictions defined by the United States government. Therefore we had to do theology in other forms than rational reflections. We sang and preached our theology in worship and other sacred contexts. The central meaning disclosed in these non-rational sources is found in both their form and content and is identical with *freedom* and *hope*.

The influence of the Black Church and its central theme of freedom and hope can be seen in the language of King's speaking and writing. Everything he said and wrote sounds like a Black sermon and not rational reflection. To be sure, King finished first in class at Crozer and also wrote a PhD dissertation on Henry Nelson Wieman's and Paul Tillich's conceptions of God at Boston; but it is significant to note that he did not adopt the style of theological presentation from any of his White theological mentors. He may have referred to White theologians and philosophers when he needed to explain his views to the White public, but the style of his presentation was unmistakably from the tradition of Black preaching. Like his predecessors and contemporaries in the Black Church, King preached his theology, because the theme of freedom and hope had to be reflected in the movement and rhythm of his voice, if he expected a Black congregation to take seriously his message. The eschatological hope of freedom is not only an idea to be analysed in the conceptual language of White theologians and philosophers. It is primarily an event to be experienced when God's word of freedom breaks into the lives of the gathered community through the vehicle of the sermon's oration. No one understood the relationship between style and meaning in the context of the Black

Church any better than Martin King. In the Black Church, the meaning is found not primarily in the intellectual content of the spoken word but in the *way* the word is spoken and its effect upon those who hear it. That was why King could speak on Plato, Augustine, Hegel or even Boston Personalism, about which most Blacks know nothing and care even less, and still move the congregation to tears and shouts of praise, even though they did not understand the content of his discourse. What they understood was the appropriate tone and movement of his speech which the people believe is the instrument for the coming presence of God's spirit, thereby empowering them with the hope for freedom. The people believe that freedom is coming because a foretaste of it is given in the sermon event itself. When King spoke of his dream at the 1963 March on Washington, and when he spoke of his hope that we will reach the Promised Land the night before his assassination in Memphis (April 1968), Black people did not believe him because of the cogency of his logic but rather because of the spirit of empowerment generated by the style of his sermon oration. The people believed him because they contended that they experienced in their hearts the Spirit of God's liberating presence.

In addition to the spoken and written style of King's theology pointing towards freedom and hope, the same theme is also found in the *content* of his message. The influence of the Black Church on the content of King's theology is not easy to demonstrate. Anyone can easily notice the influence of the Black Church on King's sermonic delivery and in the form of his writings. But that is not the case with the content of his message, since he does not explicitly refer to the Black Church. What is clear, however, is that the central themes of freedom and hope do define the content of King's life and message. It is summarised in his March on Washington speech.

> I have a dream that one day . . . the sons of former slaves and the sons of former slaveholders will be able to sit down together at the table of brotherhood. . . .
> With this faith we will be able to transform the jangling discords of our nation into a beautiful symphony of brotherhood. With this faith we will be able to work together, to pray together, to struggle together, to go to jail together, to stand up for freedom together, knowing that we will be free one day.[8]

The words were spoken in 1963 but few of us today can speak with the confidence of Martin King, because events since that time are difficult to reconcile with King's optimism. Between 1965 and 1968, even King had to move away from the optimism defined in the 1963 Washington speech, because his sermons and speeches did not dislodge the entrenchment of White power as he appeared to think. But despite the failure of his sermons and speeches to move Whites to change the social, political, and economic arrangements, the content of his message of freedom and hope did move Blacks to action. Without the response of the Black Church people, King would have had his hope for freedom destroyed, because even liberal Whites seemed incapable of embodying the hope and freedom about which he preached.

In the Black Church, King knew that the people had a hope that stretched back to the beginnings of the Black Christian community in the late eighteenth and early nineteenth centuries. All he had to do was restate that hope for freedom in the songs and language of the people, and the people would respond to the content of the message. That was why King used the language of the so-called 'Negro spirituals' in his sermons in Black churches. King's sermons always contained the hope for freedom, and he always related it to his current struggles to attain freedom in this world. But when it seemed as if freedom was difficult to realise in this world, Martin King did not despair but moved its meaning to an eschatological realm as defined by the Black Church's claim that 'the Lord will make a way somehow'. The night before he was assassinated (3 April 1968), King, in a Black Church worship service, restated that hope with the passion and certainty so typical of the Black preacher.

I don't know what will happen now. We have got difficult days ahead, but it doesn't matter with me, because I've been on the mountain top. Like anyone else, I would like to live a long life. But I'm not concerned with that. I just want to do God's will, and He has allowed me to go up the mountain.[9]

King's emphasis on the eschatological hope of freedom, as defined by 'the mountain top', was not derived from White theologians and philosophers, but rather from his own religious tradition. These words of faith and hope were derived from the Black people's struggle to overcome their pain and suffering. People who have not lived in the context of nearly 400 years of slavery and suffering are not likely to express an eschatological hope of freedom. Hope in God's coming eschatological freedom is always derived from the suffering of people who are seeking to establish freedom on earth but have failed to achieve it to their perception of their humanity. In Martin King's failure to establish freedom in his existing present, he prevented despair from becoming the defining characteristic of his life by looking forward to God's coming, eschatological freedom. Although he had to face the threat of death daily, King denied that it had the last word, for he said in the previously quoted sermon:

I see the Promised Land. I may not get there with you, but I want you to know tonight that we as a people will get to the Promised Land. I am happy tonight that I am not worried about anything. I'm not fearing any man. Mine eyes have seen the glory of the coming of the Lord.[10]

Notes

1. See especially Kenneth L. Smith and Ira G. Zepp, Jr, *Search for the Beloved Community: The Thinking of Martin Luther King, Jr.* (Valley Forge 1975) and the forthcoming text of John J. Ansbro *The Mind of Martin Luther King, Jr.* (Maryknoll, New York 1982). King's biographers make a similar assumption. See especially David L. Lewis *King: A Critical Biography* (Baltimore 1970). Martin King himself is partly responsible for this one-sided interpretation of his thinking because he seldom refers to the Black Church as the source of his theology. See especially his 'Pilgrimage to Non-violence' in *Stride Toward Freedom: The Montgomery Story* (New York 1958), pp. 90-107.

2. See especially his response to Black Power radicals in *Where Do We Go From Here: Chaos or Community?* (Boston 1967), Chapter II.

3. Marx, 'The German Ideology' in *The Marx-Engels Reader* ed. Robert C. Tucker, Second Edition, (New York 1978), pp. 158, 165.

4. For information regarding Richard Allen and the African Methodist Episcopal Church, see Carol V. R. George *Segregated Sabbaths: Richard Allen and the Rise of Independent Black Churches, 1760-1840* (New York 1973).

5. Quoted in John J. Ansbro *The Mind of Martin Luther King, Jr.* p. 89.

6. King 'Facing the Challenge of A New Age' an address delivered at the First Annual Institute on Non-violence and Social Change, Montgomery, Alabama, December 1956, in *Phylon* #8 (1957) p. 33.

7. Quoted in Ansbro *The Mind of Martin Luther King Jr.* p. 90.

8. Martin King, Jr. 'I Have A Dream' in *The Voice of Black America: Major Speeches by Negroes in the United States, 1797-1971* ed. Philip S. Foner (New York 1972) p. 974.

9. King 'I See the Promised Land', *ibid.* p. 1109.

10. *Ibid.*

Georges Casalis

Theology Under the Sign
of Martyrdom: Dietrich Bonhoeffer

HANGED ON 9 April 1945 at Flossenbürg, Dietrich Bonhoeffer (DB) is incontestably a martyr theologian; he is not—far from it—a theologian of martyrdom. This could well be meaningful: he whose death was the ultimate witness to a life of faith, he whose faith communicated at death this exceptional character of witness rendered to the Crucified and Resurrected Lord[1] could well leave to others, to the whole Christian community, the responsibility of passing the value judgment qualifying him as a martyr; the theology of martyrdom, consequently, could be elaborated by those who, far from being distant spectators, would not, however, be led to pay the price of blood *in odium fidei.* . . .

'It is remarkable that the symbol of the cross, that recalls the death of Jesus, has been the most primitive and the most constant of Christian symbols. It is already surprising that a religious community gathers around a sign which attests the death of its founder, instead of gathering round one of the many symbols which, in the Mediterranean world, attested the Resurrection. Why this reference to a penultimate event and not to the ultimate event, although solidly believed and confessed? Why this accent placed on death? To brandish the sign of the cross was to affirm that he who was recognised as "kyrios" had suffered the fate of a criminal and that this fate had been inflicted on him on the responsibility of the man who, in Rome, had had himself called "kyrios". There was a triple provocation:

'A political provocation in the affirmation that the "kyrios" of the world had suffered like a robber.

'An eschatological provocation, in the confession of the crucified Jesus as "Messiah", "Christ" of God.

'A religious provocation, in the recognition as "God" or "kyrios" of a condemned criminal. . . .

'In rallying under the sign of the cross, they exposed themselves simultaneously to the blows of religion, power and culture. . . . The death of God gives its meaning to the death of man, in so far as man agrees to die as God dies, to reproduce, to a certain degree, the death of God in his own death. . . .'

These extracts from Georges Crespy's masterly study *La Mort de Dieu comme problème théologique*[2] take very exactly into account—and this is remarkable!—both the spirituality and the historical destiny of DB. The fact is that the whole of the latter's short life took place under the sign of a theological question which is constantly reflected in a never-achieved existential quest: that for the coherence between theory and practice,[3] between what is thought and lived, or rather: between the advance of the living Christ through space and time of the world and the style of life of those who, as disciples, claim to follow him. On the occasion of the baptism of his godson, his little nephew Dietrich W. R. Bethge, he wrote, in May 1944, extraordinary phrases of prophetic lucidity: 'We have lived too much in thought and have believed that it is possible to ensure in advance, by examining all the eventualities, the outcome of any action whatsoever, so that in the end it happens by itself. Now, we have learned, a little late, that it is not thought, but the sense of responsibility that lies at the origin of action. You will discover a new relation between thought and involvement. You will only think what you have to respond to by action. Thought was often for us the luxury of the spectator, for you it will be entirely at the sevice of action. "Not every one that saith unto me, Lord, Lord . . . but he that doeth the will of my Father . . ." (Matt. 7:21).'[4] This was a quarter of a century in advance of the procedures of the 'inductive' theologies; to be exact, that of the theologians 'of liberation'. . . .

As has been noted: the involvement and the action in question here are strictly qualified: it is the will of the Father which is their *raison d'être* and standard; no human discretion rules them, but an obedience which, contrary to the accusations often levelled against DB in Barthian circles, has nothing 'legalist' about it. It is in fact a question of the dynamics of grace and this is in a direct line from the Luther of the treatise *Of the Liberty of a Christian Man*: 'A Christian is a free master of all things and is subject to no one. A Christian is a bondsman in all things and he is subject to all.'[5] The freedom of life in Christ, as proclaimed by the Word and the sign of baptism, implies a movement towards a closer and closer conformity to him who is always and simultaneously source of eternal life, openness of every human being to the 'final' dimensions and impulse towards innumerable services to the benefit of persons and groups engaged in the 'penultimate' combats of history. To convince oneself that this was at the heart of DB's theological existence one need only reread the thundering challenges which open *The Price of Grace* (1937) and which were to find their full development in the *Ethics* (1940-1943, published 1949). Grace 'costs, because it calls for obedience; it is grace because it calls for obedience to Jesus Christ; it costs, because it is, for man, at the price of his life; it is grace because, then only, it makes man a gift of life . . .'. This price to be paid—but for which life is not given as a gift—this loss of self, but for which one does not find oneself, is the very essence of the spirituality of martyrdom (see Mark 8:34 ff. and *passim*). This does not mean that DB, contrary to what was said at the beginning of this article, would have been a theologian of martyrdom—at any rate, it certainly seems that except for rare moments of despair, he had not envisaged this eventuality for himself; on the other hand he was, from the outset, a passionate supporter of evangelical radicalism, which would not exclude the possibility of martyrdom.

This latter looms to the extent that, for DB, conformity to Christ excludes any conformism, in particular with regard to all the other claimants to the title and powers of 'kyrios'. Also, as indicated in the analysis by Georges Crespy quoted above, it was not long before he became the object of the declared hostility of the official Church (religion), of the National Socialist State (politics), and of the university (culture). As we know: by a conjunction of circumstances still not clear to us, he found himself at the microphone in a State radio broadcast, on 1 February 1933, two days after Hitler took power. There it was that he pronounced the unpardonable words: 'The Führer, if he lets himself be carried away by those he leads into being regarded as an idol—and whoever is led by him will always have this hope—then the concept of "Führer" will slip more and more into that of seducer [Verführer]. . . . The Führer and the authority which deify themselves hold God up to ridicule.'[6] The broadcast was cut before these sentences could go out, but the speaker was marked; he was never to be lost sight of again.

What henceforth characterised DB's actions was that theological reflection was inseparable from a constantly prophetic reading of events. And here one is continually astonished: the great bourgeois, heir to a long and very solid aristocratic tradition, the honest 'conservative', in politics even more than in theology—and Hanfried Müller, a theologian from the GDR, makes this a major criticism: that he battled for the restoration of the 'good old Germany' and not for the establishment of a socialist republic which, in 1945, was to be set up, thanks to the arrival of the troops of atheist Communism, against all the 'spiritual forces', whether accomplices of the Third Reich, or resisting it[7]—DB then, because of or in spite of the family ideology and his ambiguous relations with the ruling class, became one of the most lucid, acute analysts of the course of events which overtook Germany and Europe. This is based quite logically on his criticism of religion and on his prisoner's intuition: the need to promote a 'non-religious' interpretation of Christian concepts, to lead to an evangelical, non-religious faith and existence. What does this mean? With several political militant theologians of the present time, with Dorothee Sölle in the forefront, I have reached the following conviction: Bonhoefferian criticism of religion comprises three dimensions: (a) employing Feuerbachian dismantling procedures: religion is the self-glorification of man, the process by which he hypostasises himself. Hence, for DB: 'no religion, revelation' and this consequence: 'The grace which costs is the incarnation of God.'[8] It is the kenosis which becomes the cipher of true humanity; no longer like Athanasius and the Orientals: 'God made himself man in order that man may become God', but rather: 'God made himself man—with all that implies of renunciation and death!—in order that man, in return, can become solidary and responsible man.' (b) Religion is therefore the most certain means invented by man to escape from the world which was entrusted to him and to betray it. The Gospel, in which, like Barth, he views the end of all religion, is, on the contrary, by very reason of the contemporaneity and 'wordliness' of God it attests, the advent of a humanity totally immersed in the human. It is, to employ Lutheran categories yet again, the end of the *securitas* illusively procured by the institutional rites and the birth of *certitudo*, life risked in search of Jesus Christ who is prepared for anything, including the death of his son, in order that men and women might live in hope of the happiness which is the ultimate aim of creation and of all political action. It is the visible existence of the disciples in the world which manifests the historical and eschatological intention of the God of life. (c) What makes all the religious categories and labels intolerable is the naked immediacy produced by political involvement. Is it an accident that, the deeper he entered into the preparation of the conspiracy, the further he drew away from ecclesiastical institutions, including the 'confessing Church', which he saw as much more worried about their own preservation than about exercising their ministry of sentinel, of watching over the people entrusted to them (Niemöller to Hitler, in 1937) and over the peace of a world in mortal danger? Faith, a-religious Christianity, are unavoidable facts for Christians involved up to the neck—up to the running noose which was to strangle them!—in the battle for the defeat of all those who use the title of 'kyrios' for the death and not, which is their only *raison d'être*, for the life of the multitudes in the 'penultimate' where justice, freedom and peace augur and hasten the coming of the 'last' realities. The adult, i.e., *politically* aware and active, Christian is the man who re-presents the practice of Christ, the suffering and death of God in secularised life, in creative, promising solidarity with all those suffering oppression under abusive and murderous powers. The hard school of the Resistance led him, as so many others, to a total identification with his contemporaries, to understand himself, in a decisive way, as 'man for others' (in the name and in the movement of Christ) and to confess, not only 'Jesus does not call to a new religion, but to life', but also: 'The Christian is not a *homo religiosus*, but quite simply a man, as Jesus, unlike John the Baptist, was a man. The Christian is of this world. . . .'[9] It is then, and then only, he says, that one can discover what happiness is and begin to enjoy life. All this was written while staring at the walls of a cell, under bombardment and faced with a very uncertain future.

Identification: the first to denounce on the radio the fatal consequences of the cult of the Führer, he was also the first, from April 1933, to take a stand against the anti-Semitic laws of 7 April. And in contrast to many theologians and to the 'confessing Church' itself, he did not do it against the prohibition placed on Judaeo-Christians to remain members of the Christian community, but against the marginalisation, discrimination and destruction of the Jewish minority within the national community. There, too, he gave proof of an exceptional prophetic clear-sightedness. Independently of his personal relations, he refused to keep away at all from his Jewish compatriots; he considered himself naturally as one of them. But—and this is not the least surprising—although he identified himself, even to the risk of 'uniformisation', with the Jews and with the conspirators of 20 July, he did so without ever losing the sense of his specific Christian identity. Rather, it is because he was profoundly, totally rooted in Christ who identified fully with him, that he could himself effect the same renunciation, join in total solidarity the others in their distress, without losing—on the contrary, in finding every day more clearly—what is the very heart of the existence of the disciple following in the steps of, and in imitation of, his master.

Awareness of the price of grace, prophetic reading of the contemporary historical reality, identification without loss of identity, corresponding in daily practice to the least details of theological conviction, such are the characteristics of the given life of DB. Convinced that all this was only possible through mercy, i.e., through the pardon ceaselessly asked and received of God, he was one of those 'saints' whose whole existence consists of communicating around them the overflowing of eternal life already manifested in them today.

Others since him: Martin Luther King, Oscar Arnulfo Romero, also my 'little' colleague, Luc Bovon, assassinated on 30 October 1981 at his home near Paris, because he had identified unreservedly with the prisoners of the central prison of Fleury-Mérogis, whose chaplain he was, because he had decided once and for all never to close to them the door of his heart and, therefore, of his house: acceptance of the price to be paid for the marvellous and demanding grace, analysing the causes of delinquency and of the shortcomings of the prison system, to the day when one of his freed brothers, overcome by an attack of madness, plunged a knife in his heart.

9 April 1945 to 30 October 1981: execution, assassination, martyrdom, add nothing to these demands; a final seal is placed on them, the death of the martyr reminds the Church that the Resurrected Lord is in agony—in the world and for it. It is for the Christian community to receive the testimony of blood and to give glory because it is living 'surrounded by such a great host of witnesses'.

Translated by Della Couling

Notes

1. O. Semmelroth 'Martyrium' in *Mysterium Salutis* (Freiburg—Basle—Vienna 1969).

2. Georges Crespy 'Essais sur la situation actuelle de la foi' in *Cogitatio fidei* 48 (Paris 1970) pp. 93 ff.

3. Cf. R. Mengus 'Théorie et Pratique chez DB' *Théologie historique* 50 (Paris 1978).

4. DB *Résistance et soumission* (Geneva 1967) p. 137.
5. Martin Luther *Oeuvres* (French translation, Geneva 1966) vol. 2.
6. E. Bethge *DB, eine Biographie* (Munich 1967) pp. 307 ff.
7. Hanfried Müller *Von der Kirche zur Welt* (Leipzig 1961).
8. DB 'Prédication du 11 mars 1928, à Barcelone' *Opera omnia* (in German) V, pp. 417-423.
9. R. Mengus, in the article cited in note 3, p. 424.

Daniel Berrigan

Resist and Renew: The Church at the Brink

AS I write this, my older brother Jerome, a teacher and father of four, has been released from prison; he committed an act of resistance against nuclear war at the Pentagon. My brother Philip and I are presently free on appeal, having been sentenced to three to ten years for destruction of nuclear warheads in 1980.

The rhythm of life for us and for our friends is by and large this; in and out of the Pentagon, the White House, the military bases and think tanks, in and out of courts and jails. This has been our story for a long time.

From the point of view of the State, we are Christians who are literally beyond rehabilitation.

Yet there is another story to be told. We are also Americans. In our groups are professionals, teachers, lawyers, doctors, parents, seminarians, monks, nuns, priests. We are middle class, white, university educated. We take our place with a certain modest anonymity, in the ranks of citizens; we have no great objection to obeying laws, if such are of benefit to the common life, good order and so on. And we are invariably and continually, in trouble with the law of the land. Our story is both old and disconcertingly new. For us, it is almost two decades old.

The story implies (and here I will speak for myself) the recovery of a very old and crucial tradition, one which was denied us in our childhood, in military service (it goes without saying); more, in seminary and Church teaching. The tradition was literally drummed out of us by the war drums of our culture and world. It was denied us by a persistent, all but irresistible myth; that of the 'virtuous', 'necessary' war; which is to say, any and every war in which our country took sides, any and every war in which our Church concurred.

The nuclear arms race sums up our predicament, threatening as it does to bring the human adventure itself to a fiery halt. The race is quite literally and coldly, a race towards extinction; it thus sums up, in its ethos and mythology, the irrationality of war itself; an irrationality which so called 'limited' war had muted. We are now monotonously informed that if 'sufficiently armed' (though 'sufficiently', like the appetite of a distrait beast, has no limit), we shall stave off the war that looms above; by continually piling up fuels, we shall trim the fires of Armageddon.

According to this reasoning, we avoid war by preparing for war. We make war less likely by preparing for an (unlikely) war. We think steadfastly about the unthinkable;

85

and the unthinkable somehow is exorcised. The creation of a war econony, a warlike climate of opinion, a Draconian attitude towards political and religious deviants, the imposition of ruinous war taxes on all, a staggering allocation of resources to weaponry and weapons research—all this, we are instructed, is a multiple form of war prevention. By such arrangements, we are inoculated with a kind of preventive poison, immunised against nuclear war.

Thus goes the theory, huckstered with a straight face, far and wide. That the theory, by any measure available, is plain madness—this makes little practical difference. For in the venerable Marat Sade institution, the war-making State, a collective madhouse, there is little room for the intrusion of diagnosis or healing. That world, guarded, isolated, self-sufficient, sets its own criteria and conduct, its own morality and mission; it must be added, writes its own Bible and sacred signs. The madhouse can count, by and large, on a network of supportive institutions, partly sane, partly in bondage to madness, which lie in its penumbra. Such are the university (it does research into functional madness) the law courts and prisons (these determine punishment for the wilfully sane), the economy (to determine who shall prosper and who be declared disposable), the Church (to celebrate rites of insanity, to bless godlike guns) the family (to produce a lockstep populace). In such ways, the madhouse decides the livelihood, advancement, professional status, of vast numbers of researchers and workers. The madhouse management has life and death powers over those under its direct control, and its 'outpatients'; they are recruited in youth, commanded to kill and maim, have their own lives snatched away. Management decisions create immense tundras of misery, defeat, psychic dislocation and despair; they also create a feverish, instant affluence.

Truly, this world of closed doors, immense power, secrecy and public duplicity, this world which is not quite at war and just as certainly never at peace—this is no world of ordinary mortals, but a world of self-intoxicated giants, of mysterious technocrats, dreamers, myth-makers, shamins. Obey them you must, resist them at risk.

Into such a world, Christianity intrudes.

The believers come as strangers, outsiders. We are the alienated. We literally cannot make sense of such a world. More; we have no intention of 'adjusting'; a finicky sense of ourselves, developed over the midnight lamp, keeps us at distance; we have read the gospels too closely. We find there no blessing on war; we find suffering, legal sanctions, death, as the natural outcome of a faith that 'goes too far'. We do not know what the phrase means; indeed we suspect we have not gone far enough. But we have come this far, a certain distance; and we will not budge nor give up.

America is our country; our destiny will be worked out here. We are responsible for the place where we were born; responsible, among other things, for its wars. We undertake this responsibility as we undertake our faith in Christ; these are, in effect, but one credo. In accord with this faith, this singleness of understanding, we recall that the saints of Revelation cry out from beneath the altar their 'How long?'. And in the Acts of the Apostles, we read not only that the early Christians were persecuted, but that they rejoiced to be accounted 'worthy to suffer for the Name'. Also that they returned again and again to the forbidden teaching, and were repeatedly apprehended, flogged, threatened, held in public scorn. Thus does a sacred calling imply the most brutal secular consequence. The faith has 'gone too far'.

To understand our situation today *vis-à-vis* the war-making State, one must take a close look at Church–State realities. In a society like ours, there are few who can draw clear lines between sacred and secular. Until recently, the common ploy was to keep things publicly vague and privately convenient. One could put matters academically; complementary and interpenetrating powers. A certain number of citizens also happen to be believers; their belief is in the nature of an appendix to citizenship, no great matter; if troublesome, easily excised. Citizen-believers are foggily persuaded that a ticket to the good life here below does double duty; it grants admission also to the kingdom of God. A charade is played out by officials of both powers, Church and State. Cardinals, generals, blessed, cozened, praised, conferred gifts, worshipped, urged 'good citizenship' and 'church attendance'. By and large, once the smog of rhetoric was penetrated, each talked the same language, drew on the same debased myths, shared like ambitions. They blessed conformity and moral mediocrity, made of the Church the sedulous ape of secular violence. In the process, they conferred on the makers and breakers of humanity, a credible (although totally spurious) image of civic uprightness, even of holiness.

We were locked tight in a horrid nightmare, I know of no other way of describing our plight, from our youth through the early Sixties. We were locked into America; it makes little difference that our prison was graced with Gothic arches, that Gregorian chant sounded its labyrinths. Locked in we were; and in whose hand was the key?

The State's main business was war; we were prisoners of war. Did our Church hold the key to our freedom? If it did, it withheld our freedom in its right arm, which was in effect, the spiritual arm of the State. You cannot bless war, we learned to our sorrow; and with the same arm, free the prisoners.

At a recent workshop held in New York, an admiral from the Pentagon spoke on nuclear arms and conscience. He introduced himself as a Christian who had heard repeatedly the call of Christ to the ministry of the Church. But he averred, he felt an even stronger call to remain where he was, 'serving my country according to my oath, which concludes with the phrase, "so help me God" '.

He was adamant on this point; righteous and fully assured as a novice. To serve his country was to serve Christ. His story is of more than passing interest. The admiral is an officer in a nuclear navy. He passed two years, as he recounted, with his finger on the nuclear button, in one of the great secret command centres. 'I knew that in the navy, we had seven minutes before an enemy missile struck; that in the army the time was extended to half an hour. And I was willing, day or night, to transmit the message to the president, recommending that we launch missiles. So help me God.'

It must be added that the admiral appeared in no wise troubled or of two minds. To the contrary. His conviction endued him with passion and forthrightness. Doomsday at centre eye, he never flinched. Faced with his awesome duty, he appeared as a very model, a defender of the faith. The United States, he asserted, was the divine instrument for the protection of God's people. If God should demand that America undertake a final showdown, then so be it; for God wills it. So help me God.

We have here a new twist on the ancient Apocalypse. Biblical images referring to the last days, images of joy, mutuality, unity, are submerged. More, they are declared null and void. Banquet of the kingdom, nuptials of Christ and bride, paradise restored, hidden treasure uncovered, sowing come to harvest—none of these. It is to a purely secular, violent, conclusive Armageddon we are summoned. We are in fact commanded to summon it, to bring it to pass. Final catastrophe rules the Christian imagination. It wears the guise of civic and religious duty. It can imagine only—war; a warrior Christ, a war to end all wars. This imagination is functional, efficient; it enlists all, from admirals to hoplites, in the torching of the world. What might formerly be regarded as a fantastic image of diseased minds or science fiction *aficionados*, is by now, stone-cold fact, discussed as probability, taken in account, planned for day after day. The medium is by now one with the message; the ideology has created the weaponry; the weapons underscore the ideology in blood and fire.

Another aspect of the admiral's world vision merits attention. It is his view of the end time.

Let us indulge in a word of cold comfort. In spite of all Christian crimes—colonialism, wars, high piracy—crimes whose catalogue was created in the commission—in spite of all this, Christian theology has held with a stubbornness it can never quite explain—to the mysterious character of the end of things. Questioned as to time and place and manner, the Church has responded with Christ, a simple 'I do not know'. Thus the Church announced not only a saving ignorance, chastening alike to magic and the itch of frivolity. She also declared something both precious and positive. Like this: 'My not-knowing is a tribute to the truth, God-knows. And in the divine One, God-knowing is God-acting. As the end time is in God's hands (and if this is true, all time rests in God's hands) so is the occasion, manner, image (as all occasions, manners, images). Therefore something momentous follows. The fate of the living and the unborn, along with all temporal outcomes and eventualities, judgments, restitutions, healings, including every human, civil, national arrangement arrived at along the way—all this must be considered provisory. Every secular decision, including the most momentous, compassionate, obviously virtuous, must be performed in fear and trembling. At every hour, every nation State is summoned to judgment—and found wanting, at least in the essential and final sense, that it is not the kingdom of God and cannot be. For a claim rests on every human, at every point of history. It is a claim which no admiral, shah, president, junta, pope, can pre-empt. Christ owns us. We belong elsewhere.'

That the claim has often been pre-empted is no news. Christian action has invariably belied Christian faith. This is a matter of history; the bloodstained face of victims, the commissars of religious power. Indeed it could be ventured that the American admiral, in his mad purity and Promethean scope, is no new phenomenon. He comes from somewhere, from familiar ground. He speaks a tongue that awakens memories, resonances. He claims the world, in Christ's name, and the world's people, chattels, ransom, hostages of empire. The empire is the kingdom of God, revealed in one blinding, world-enveloping nuclear flash.

The admiral is thus one with the Grand Inquisitors, the colonial enslavers, the generals in the sanctuaries (as recently in tortured Argentina, at the pope's mass). With a mad moral ictus as old as the first plunging of the cross on 'infidel soil', the admiral comes ashore in the twentieth century, to announce, through nuclear sword and cross, the ancient evangel, death the saviour. Thy kingdom come—at last. And its name (formerly New Spain, New France, New England)—is America. So help me God.

Call it disease or displaced imagination—it comes perhaps to the same thing. The biblical vision of world and history, which touches our hearts as a profoundly telling, sensible, mystical vision of the human itself, the human blessed, vindicated, crowned—the vision is displaced. God is a displaced person, loses place. What seizes the centre cannot be called human at all; more exactly it is the inhuman, the demonic. Concretely, in our age, it is technique in service of death.

God loses place, God as displaced person.

Does God also lose face, given so mad a world? Let us say only that in Christ, God has many faces, many mirrors held to the world, reflecting back, not the inert or fatalistic or death ridden. Rather the human drama, tragic beyond telling, criminal, conscienceless, power without advocacy, powerlessness without recourse. And more; for the mirror does not merely reflect, a rear view. It is vatic, it speaks up—it tells of an end of things, an outcome, a righting of wrongs, a warning to the wrongdoers; and derision towards the nations, their inflated pride, their aping of God. 'Pharoah and his chariots, all drowned in the sea.'

The admiral is not easily forgotten, he struck deep. His faith seemed strong as our own, if not stronger (we being so often assailed with doubt, second thoughts and third, fears, dread, longing, backward glances). He seemed to live, and envision dying, under a better star and dispensation than we. He had clear landmarks, he exuded confidence, single-mindedness. He drew a line with the blade of his sword; let the world take notice; God is on our side.

The world takes notice. The admiral is a serious man. There is no need of reminders; My Lai, Hiroshima, domestic slavery, genocide against native Americans. The admiral is also American, he means what he says, says exactly what he means. He has created, unlike many renowned theologians, an admirable unity between praxis and word.

What does all this come to? Why does the admiral's faith seem to me a form of despair, bankrupt, chauvinistic, heretical, contemptuous of the God of the living, biblically illiterate? If I seek to discover why my judgment is so sweeping (and at the same time, solitary) a few clues come to mind. The first has been referred to—the destruction of biblical variety by the obsessive image. Under great pressure from a culture, inheriting a religion of flag and altar, required to state religious belief as a condition of entering military academy, pronouncing an oath of civic loyalty as a condition of officer status, placed in charge of doomsday weaponry— in such circumstances, the admiral's capacity for truth, for judgment, for sanity, is mercilessly tumbled and jumbled. Dense and awry, a centre coalesces; its name is civic religion, it lives under oath to the State, it is inured to megadeath as a fact of life.

The new centre is, in fact, a Christian 'new man', in the ultimate, anti-Marxist sense—a creation at least as dangerous as its opposite number. We have also called this new centre, this centre of storms, morally awry. Displaced historically, obsessively and imperially Christian, the admiral takes the history of war, of Christian war, for his only history, for Christian history. The crusades, the Inquisition, colonial wars, imperial wars, world wars—they are all Christian wars. No other Christian history is worth considering. Given the world, given enemies, sinners, infidels, Communists, the only permissable Christian conduct is—war.

Thus at a stroke, the stroke of a sword, the first three hundred years of Christian history are disposed of. The books are burned; including, it must be said, the book of the gospels. The stern prohibition against killing that held firm for so long, the prohibition against military service and war taxes—of these the admiral knows nothing, or as nearly nothing as to make no difference. The presumption is that our true history began with our first (virtuous) war. Every war since has been laudable, even blessed, in proportion as Christians took part, raised weapons and standards for an asperges, were served by national chaplains, partook of the Eucharist, were assured of salvation on the battlefield. 'Dulce et decorum.' The pagan poet could not have put matters more beautifully, more ethically, on behalf of Christians.

Thus the admiral represents not only the awesome power and prestige of the nuclear super State, an ethos which justifies nuclear arms and, quite probably, nuclear war. He also powerfully reinforces the ethos, gives it religious coloration, language, infuses it with all but irresistible majesty: 'The whole world followed after the beast. . . . It was given the beast to wage war against the sants, and to defeat them.'

If the admiral is confident, it is because he knows he does not stand alone, brandishing the nuclear blade in the name of Christ. The spirit that drives him animates others as well; at the peak of the American military, he is in goodly company. These masters of fate assemble regularly in suburban homes for prayer and worship, they are fervent churchgoers, the convictions of the admiral are, by and large, the convictions of all.

Thus the fate of the nations, the children, the unborn, the very pith and meaning of the human adventure—these have become chips in a stupendous game; a game in which winning and losing are not only tactically absurd considerations, but are actually deemed irrelevant by the players. 'God wills it!' is their cry. Their game is serious, they are stern and austere as martyrs before the fires, a hallucinatory transcendence shines in their eyes. If need be, if a sign is given, they will launch the missiles. The end of the world will be a religious act.

Contributors

MAURICE BARTH, OP, was born in 1916 at Mulhouse, France. He did his theological studies at Le Saulchoir and was ordained in 1944. He was successively student chaplain at Strasburg, director of the Centre International Saint-Bernard in Berlin between 1952-1955, and director of the Centre International Maydieu in Paris between 1967-1973. He is a member of many committees of solidarity with the Third World and is currently responsible for the department of the Rights of Man at CIMADE (Service oecumenique d' entraide) in Paris. He is president of Amitiés franco-chiliennes and of Solidarité Amérique Centrale—Oscar Romero, as well as being France's delegate on the Commission des Droits de l'homme d'El Salvador. He has published several articles in French reviews and weeklies about Latin America, and is co-author of *Salvador—Oscar Romero et son peuple* (1982).

THEOFRIED BAUMEISTER, OFM, born in 1941 at Recklinghausen, Germany, joined the Franciscans in 1960 and was ordained priest in 1967. He continued his studies at Münster University, where he gained his degree in theology in 1971 and in 1976 his *Habilitation* in the field of early Church history, patrology and Christian archaeology. He has conducted research in Rome and Egypt. Since 1976 he has been professor of early Church history at Mainz and at the same time guest lecturer at the Franciscan and Capuchin study centre at Münster. His publications on the subject of the present article have been: *Martyr invictus. Der Märtyrer als Sinnbild der Erlösung in der Legende und im Kult der frühen koptischen Kirche* (1972), and *Die Anfänge der Theologie des Martyriums* (1980). Other works are concerned in particular with the history of piety and devotion in the early Church.

LEONARDO BOFF was born in Brazil in 1938 and now teaches dogmatic and systematic theology at Petrópolis. He is editor of *Revista Eclesiástica Brasileira* and of the Brazilian edition of *Concilium*. He is author of *Jesus Christ Liberator* (1972) and several other books including *The Maternal Face of God* (1980). His latest work is a study of St Francis.

WALBERT BÜHLMANN, OMCap, was born in Switzerland in 1916. He is a Capuchin friar, and since 1971 has been General Secretary of the Capuchin Order's missionary programme. He has published many books, including *The Coming of the Third Church* (London 1982) and *The Chosen Peoples* (London 1982).

PEDRO CASALDÁLIGA, a Catalan, was born in Spain in 1928 and is a Claretian missionary. He has lived in Brazil since 1968 and in 1971 was ordained bishop of São Félix do Araguaia, in the Matto Grosso. He is a poet and writer whose books include *I believe in Justice and Hope, Tierra nuestra, libertad (Our Land, Freedom)* and, in collaboration with others, the *Missa da terra sem males* (Mass for a World Without Evils) and *Missa dos Quilombos* (a Black liberation mass).

GEORGES CASALIS, born in 1917 in Paris, is a Protestant theologian and a member of the Reformed Church of France. He has been in succession: General Secretary of the

French Federation of Student Christian Associations; country pastor (Vendée); in the ecumenical mission in Berlin (1945-1950); pastor of the Lutheran Church in Alsace and in Lorraine; since 1961, professor of practical theology and hermeneutics at the Protestant Institute of Theology (Faculty of Paris). He is a member of the Commission on Social, Economic and International Affairs of the Protestant Federation of France, and for the time being a member of the organising team of the Ecumenical Institute for the Development of Peoples. He has given courses in foreign universities in Europe and in the Third World. His recent publications include: *Kénose et Histoire* (1970); *Lectures bibliques des protestants* (1970); *Prédication, acte politique* (1970); *Protestantisme* (1976); *Les Idées justes ne tombent pas du ciel* (1977); *Libération et religion* (1981).

FRANCISCO CLAVER has been bishop of the Prelature of Malaybalay since 1969. He had gained a STL from Woodstock College (Maryland, USA) in 1962, and a PhD (Anthropology) from the University of Colorado (Boulder, Colorado, USA) in 1973. Recently he wrote 'L'Eglise des Philippines: entre la compromission et le prophetisme' in *Etudes* (April 1980) 515-529.

JAMES H. CONE received his BA from Philander Smith College in Little Rock, Arkansas, his BD from Garrett Theological Seminary, and his MA and PhD from Northwestern University in Evanston, Illinois. He has also been awarded the LLD from Edward Waters College in Jacksonville, Florida and the LHD From Philander Smith. He is at present Charles A. Briggs Professor of Systematic Theology at Union Theological Seminary, New York. He has published many articles and several books. His books include: *Black Theology and Black Power* (New York 1969); *A Black Theology of Liberation* (New York 1970); *The Spirituals and the Blues: An Interpretation* (New York 1972); *God of the Oppressed* (New York 1975); *Black Theology: A Documentary History, 1966-1979* (edited with Gayraud S. Wilmore) (1979); and *My Soul Looks Back* (Nashville, Tennessee 1982).

ABEL HERZBERG was born in September 1893 in Amsterdam of Russian parents. He obtained his degree in law at the University of Amsterdam in 1925. He joined the Dutch army during the First World War, though not yet naturalised, and practised as a lawyer in Amsterdam from 1925 till 1980, except from March 1943 till April 1945, when he was interned in various German camps, and finally, with his wife, for fifteen months in Bergen Belsen. He has received many literary prizes and official distinctions. Among his works are *Tweestromenland* (his Belsen diary), a chronicle of the persecution of the Jews, the 'Memoirs of King Herod'.

ENDA McDONAGH is a priest of the Archdiocese of Tuam and professor of moral theology at Maynooth. His latest book, *The Making of Disciples* (Gill and Macmillan), was published in November 1982.

JUAN HERNÁNDEZ PICO, SJ, is forty-six and is a naturalised Guatemalan, having been born in Bilbao. He entered the Society of Jesus in 1953 and was destined for Central America from 1957. After studies in Spain and Germany he was ordained priest in 1966 and did post-graduate work in sociology at the University of Chicago. He is a member of the Jesuit Centre for Social Investigation and Action in Central America (CIASCA), and has been its director since 1981. He is a member of the Managua-based Historical Institute of Central America (IHCA). He has contributed to: *El Salvador: Año Político 1971-72* (1973), and has written *Fe Cristiana y Revolución Sandinista en Nicaragua* (1980); *Apuntes para una Teología Nicaragüense* (1981). His articles include 'Método teológico, Cristología y Praxis política en América Latina' *ECA* 1978; 'Tesis para una comprensión del proceso político guatamalteco' *ECA* 1978; 'La oración en los procesos latinoamericanos de liberación' *Diálogo* 1979; and 'Conllevar las cargas en servicio del reino: reflexión teológica sobre la solidaridad con Centroamérica' *Christus* (1982).

JON SOBRINO, SJ, a Basque by origin, was born in 1938. He has been a Jesuit since 1956, in the Latin American province since 1957. He was ordained in 1969 and lives in El Salvador. He holds a degree in philosophy and a master's degree in engineering from the University of St Louis, and a doctorate in theology from Frankfurt. His major published works are *Christology at the Crossroads* (1978) and *La Resurrección de la verdadera Iglesia* (1981). Since then he has also written *Oscar Romero* (a collection of articles) and his *Jesús en América Latina* (1982) is still at the press.

DESMOND TUTU was born in October 1931 at Klerksdorp, Transvaal (South Africa). His father was a schoolteacher; his mother was relatively uneducated. He married Leah Nomalizo Tutu in 1955, and she bore him four children. He received High School education at Johannesburg Bantu High School, Western Native Township, up to Matric (1945-1950). He gained a Teacher's Diploma at Pretoria Bantu Normal College (1951-1953) in 1954—BA (UNISA). He taught at Munsieville High School, Krugersdorp between 1955-1958. He went to St Peter's Theological College, Rosettenville, Johannesburg, for ordination training between 1958-1960. He was ordained deacon in December 1960, and priest in 1961. His family went to England between 1962-1966 and lived at Golder's Green, London, whilst he was part-time curate at St Alban's, between 1962-1965. He gained a BD(Hons) (London) in 1965, and MTh (London) in 1966. He visited the Holy Land with his family en route to South Africa in 1966. He joined the staff of the Federal Theological Seminary, Alice, Cape, 1967-1969; was lecturer at the Department of Theology, UBLS, Roma, Lesotho, 1970-1972; associate director, Theological Education Fund of the World Council of Churches based in Bromley, Kent, 1972-1975. He was dean of Johannesburg, 1975-1976; bishop of Lesotho, 1976-1978; and became General Secretary, South African Council of Churches in 1978. He attended the 'Salvation Today' Conference at Bangkok, Thailand; the All Africa Conference of Churches General Assembly, Lusaka; the Anglican Consultative Council, Port of Spain; the Lambeth Conference, Canterbury. He was elected Fellow of King's College, London, in 1978. He was awarded an Honorory Doctorate of Divinity from General Theological Seminary, USA, in May 1978; an Honorary Doctorate of Civil Law from Kent University, England, in July 1978; an Honorary Doctorate of Civil Law from Harvard, USA, in July 1979; the Prix d'Athene (Onassis Foundation) in 1980; a DD by Aberdeen Unviersity, Scotland, in July 1981; a DTheol from Ruhr University, Bochum, in November 1981. He is the author of several articles and reviews as well as: *Crying in the Wilderness; J'ai aussi le doit d'exister*.

CONCILIUM

All back issues are still in print and available for sale. Orders should be sent to the publishers,

T. & T. CLARK LIMITED
36 George Street, Edinburgh EH2 2LQ, Scotland

The Von Balthasar Reader

Edited by Medard Kehl SJ and Werner Löser SJ

Professors of dogmatic theology at the Philosophical-Theological
Hochschule St Georgen in Frankfurt, West Germany

Hans Urs von Balthasar is one of the magisterial figures of contemporary theology. Over a long and immensely productive career he has demonstrated an original spiritual faculty of observation joined with a unique intellectual and religious breadth of knowledge, an intensive theological power of penetration, and a moving and often passionately moved artistic power of expression.

In 112 representative texts, the *Reader* affords a comprehensive view of the key themes of von Balthasar's life and work. Introducing the *Reader* is a 50-page 'Portrait' of von Balthasar which describes the personal encounters that have influenced him and the chief aspects of his theological achievement.

0 567 09343 3   440 pp   cased   £14·95

Available in the USA from The Crossroad Publishing Company, New York

T. & T. CLARK LTD., 36 GEORGE STREET, EDINBURGH EH2 2LQ, SCOTLAND